IS THERE
MALE
MENOPAUSE?

IS THERE MALE MENOPAUSE?

APANDISIS
α
PUBLISHING

Apandisis Publishing
105 Madison Avenue, Suite 3A
New York, New York 10016

ISBN-13: 978-1-4127-5273-2
ISBN-10: 1-4127-5273-6

Manufactured in USA

8 7 6 5 4 3 2 1

www.FYIanswers.com

Contents

Chapter One
BODY SCIENCE

Chapter Two
ANIMAL KINGDOM

Chapter Three
LOVE AND LUST

Chapter Four
ORIGINS AND TRADITIONS

Chapter Five
PEOPLE

Chapter Six
FOOD AND DRINK

Chapter Seven
PLACES

Chapter Eight
WEIRD SCIENCE AND TECHNOLOGY

Chapter Nine
HEALTH MATTERS

Chapter Ten
HISTORY

Chapter Eleven
EARTH AND SPACE

Chapter Twelve
SPORTS

Chapter Thirteen
MORE GOOD STUFF

BODY SCIENCE

Q Is there male menopause?

A Ever wonder why Clint Eastwood doesn't play tough-guy roles anymore? Maybe it's because he spends so much time behind the camera as a director. Or maybe it's something more sinister...something hormonal. That's right; we're talking about male menopause. While no one wants to picture a grown man suffering from hot flashes or blubbering his way through a rough day, the sad truth is that male menopause is a medical reality.

The first thing you should know about male menopause is that most medical professionals bristle at this colloquial name. Conventional menopause is defined by the dramatic plunge in estrogen production that women experience when they stop menstruating. So-called male menopause involves the masculine equivalent of estrogen—testosterone—but the two conditions are quite different. In men, testosterone production can slowly level off over a number of years, beginning at age forty and continuing for decades. In female menopause, estrogen levels drop radically in a relatively short period of time. Furthermore, menopause in women signifies the end of fertility. This is not necessarily the case for men: The world's oldest father was reported to have sired a child at the age of ninety-three.

In an effort to be more precise, the medical community has coined the term "andropause" to describe the hormonal issues a man begins to experience in middle age. What exactly are these issues? Many men don't exhibit any symptoms, but those whose testosterone levels dip too significantly can experience a number of unpleasant side effects.

These may include depression, exhaustion, decreased muscle mass and height, hot flashes or sweating, loss of interest in sex, impotence, and the dreaded "man-boobs" (enlarged breasts, otherwise known as gynecomastia). Yep, it's not a pretty picture, and it's time for us to face the grim possibility that Dirty Harry might not be able to hoist the old .44 Magnum the way he once did.

Since andropause is a natural part of aging, there's not much that can be done to prevent or treat it. Some men, however, maintain normal testosterone levels throughout their lives and are spared man-boobs and bouts of pathetic weeping.

So if you're a man who is approaching middle age, the question you have to ask yourself is, "Do I feel lucky?" Well, do ya, punk?

Q If a man is paralyzed from the waist down, can he still get an erection?

A The short answer is yes. Paraplegia is not an all-or-nothing state—there are myriad combinations of nerve damage that can result in the inability to move from the waist down. The particular state of the damage will determine whether a man can have an erection.

However, doctors say that it is not easy for a paraplegic to achieve and maintain an erection. And if his injuries include damage to nerves that carry sensory impulses to the brain, it's possible that he won't feel the pleasurable sensations associated with the stimulus of the penis and the resulting erection. Nevertheless, the ability to have an erection and ejaculate is important to many paraplegics, especially those who want to continue to have sexual relations or want to father children.

How do men with these injuries have sex and father children? Well, "sex" is anything you want to make it, but if you're talking about heterosexual intercourse, there is what therapists call the "stuffing" technique, in which either the man or woman manually inserts the soft penis into her vagina and she induces a "reflex erection" by moving her hips and contracting and releasing her vaginal muscles.

There are mechanical and medical means as well. A "medical vibrator" from Denmark called FertiCare is described as being considerably more intense than a standard vibrator and requires a prescription. Applied lengthwise under the penis, it can cause an involuntary reaction—an erection—and result in quick, strong orgasms. It costs anywhere from eight hundred to one thousand dollars. Those whose goal is to father a child can choose a combination of procedures in which sperm are harvested from the man's body and implanted in the woman via intrauterine insemination or *in vitro* fertilization.

The question posed here might seem simple and straightforward enough, but many of its answers are complex, just like the human body itself.

Q How many gallons of pee does the human population produce each day?

A Pee pee. Wee wee. Tinkle. Piss. Call it what you will, but everyone does it, every day. Considering there are more than 6.5 billion humans on the planet, there's definitely a whole lot of whizzle whirling around.

How much we each piddle each day depends on a lot of factors—including Big Gulp dependencies and unfortunately enlarged prostates—but we don't need to dive too deep into these issues. In healthy folks, the normal amount of urine passed each day is about equal to the amount of fluids taken in. The Mayo Clinic says for the average adult, that comes out to approximately 1.5 liters a day.

Now this isn't exact science, but to approximate how much pee the human population produces each day, all we have to do is multiply 1.5 liters by the world's population. And here's what we get: 10,016,345,882 liters, 10,016,346 kiloliters, or about 2.6 billion U.S. liquid gallons of pee per day.

Just how much tinkle are we talking? Well, if those 2.6 billion gallons of daily pee were gasoline, you could use it to fuel all the cars in Wisconsin for an entire year. Think about that the next time you point Percy at the porcelain.

Q Do people really go mad during a full moon?

A A full moon appears. People go batty. Right? Ask emergency-room workers or police officers, and they'll tell you that the number of disturbed individuals who come to their attention rises dramatically during a full moon. Or maybe not.

It's a long-held belief that a lunar effect causes "lunacy" in susceptible people—resulting in an increase in homicides, traffic accidents, suicides, kidnappings, crisis calls to emergency services, admissions to psychiatric institutions, and all kinds of other nutty things. The rationale: The earth is 80 percent water, and so is the human body. Theoretically, then, since the moon has such a dramatic effect on the tides, it could move the water in our bodies in some similar way, causing strange things to happen.

Are the stories true? Most evidence says no.

In 1996, scientists Ivan Kelly, James Rotton, and Roger Culver did a thorough examination of more than one hundred studies of lunar effects. Perhaps surprisingly, they found no significant correlation between the state of the moon and people's mental and physical conditions. When all of the statistical wrinkles had been smoothed out, there was no evidence of a rise in violence, accidents, disasters, or any other kind of strange behavior.

A study by C. E. Climent and R. Plutchik, written for *Comprehensive Psychiatry,* showed that psychiatric admissions are *lowest* during a full moon, and an examination conducted at the University of Erlangen–Nuremberg in Germany indicated no connection between suicide rates and phases of the moon. So why the myths? Perhaps people just want to believe the spooky tales, and lunar effects are tossed into movies and literature simply because they're compelling drama. Who doesn't love a good werewolf tale?

The constant reinforcement of the "full moon" message makes it much more likely that the public will accept it as proven fact. Myths also tend to stay alive if you pick and choose the data to fit the story. One murder that occurs during a full moon creates a story that can be told over and over, yet the ten homicides that happen at any other time of the month just disappear into a pile of statistics.

Renowned UCLA astronomer George O. Abell consistently dismissed claims that the moon could have a strong enough effect on the water in a human body to cause any behavioral changes. Abell pointed out that a mosquito would exert more gravitational pull on a human arm than the moon ever might.

So, is that arm-biting mosquito spooked by the moon? That's not entirely a joke, because it seems animals actually are affected by lunar activity. It might be a bit scary to read a study in the *British Medical Journal* that appears to prove there's a significant increase in bites by cats, rats, horses, and dogs when the moon is full.

Suddenly, the image of a dog howling at the moon might give you a little shiver. But a man baying at the moon? Most likely he'd be someone who's goofy all month long.

Q How old do you have to be to die of old age?

A Answering this question is like trying to catch a little ball of mercury rolling around on the floor. It just keeps slipping away.

If we take the question literally, we have to define what "dying of old age" means. For most of us, it's dying at an age when our bodies have become naturally susceptible to maladies than can end a life—primarily cancer and heart disease. When these strike at a certain age, there's less sense of fate having been cruel and unfair to us.

Or we can take the question to simply mean, "How old is old?" In other words, we skip the dying part, which is fine by us. Either way, the answer is slippery.

The definition of "old" has varied by era. In 1900 an American newborn had a life expectancy of fewer than fifty years. Today, it's eighty years or more for a woman and nearly that for a man. In 1950 the life expectancy in India was roughly thirty-two; by

2000 it had doubled. To some extent, the lower life expectancies reflected the higher risk of premature death—from disease or hunger, for example. So it doesn't mean that a fifty-year-old in 1900 was necessarily "old"—although because of poorer nutrition and less advanced medical care (among other important factors), a fifty-year-old back then was typically more enfeebled than one is today.

The fact is, "old age" is an imprecise combination of social and cultural impressions and demographic realities. As U.S. Supreme Court Justice Potter Stewart said famously of pornography in 1964, "I know it when I see it." So we could say that a person is "old" when he or she is noticeably slowed by the effects of age. The problem is, that and a quarter would have gotten you a cup of coffee in 1980.

So let's discuss some of the attempts to pin a number on old age. In the United States, sixty-five has been the traditional retirement age and when we're referred to as "senior citizens"; for a long time, it was the age when Social Security benefits kicked in. Thus, sixty-five has taken on unofficial status as the beginning of old age—"young-old age," as some gerontologists put it, splitting gray hairs as they go. For them, seventy-five is "old-old," although as people live longer and longer, eighty-five has come to be seen as truly old.

We'll leave it at that—somewhere in the neighborhood of eighty-five—and quote a bit of maudlin poetry, from American writer and businessman Samuel Ullman: "Nobody grows old merely by living a number of years. We grow old by deserting our ideals. Years may wrinkle the skin, but to give up enthusiasm wrinkles the soul."

Q Do you become fish food if you're buried at sea?

A You're swimming along looking for dinner. You're not picky—after all, you are a fish. But another helping of creatures that are lower than you on the food chain isn't going to hit the spot. You want to score new grub.

Eureka!—you spy it. It's a casket, broken open at the bottom of the ocean, with a human corpse still inside. "Get a bib," you think. "It looks like we're having seconds tonight!"

Fish, crabs, and small sea animals will go to town on a human corpse. They work so quickly that they are known to speed up the decomposition process a hundredfold. Soft parts of the face are eaten first, including the eyelids, lips, ears, eyes, nose, and mouth. Larger fish tend to dine on the torso and extremities, and sharks generally tear off eight- to ten-inch chunks of the body. (A summer rarely passes without a news story about someone in a coastal town reeling in a shark that has a human limb in its stomach.)

There are rules governing burials at sea. They are based on the Marine Protection, Research and Sanctuary Act of 1972 and are regulated according to the Clean Water Act. Human bodies committed to the deep must be at least three nautical miles from land and in water at least six hundred feet deep. Presumably, this ensures that any leftovers won't wash ashore and terrify little Johnny as he's playing in the surf.

Once a corpse is sleeping with the fishes, can you discourage the fish from immediately chowing down? You can if you fill the corpse with embalming fluid before tossing it overboard. While fish are not particularly finicky, they generally don't have a taste for formaldehyde.

These days, fish even gnaw on live bodies—and the experience can cost you good money. Some high-end spas offer treatments in which customers put their feet in small ponds that are filled with fish from Turkey called *Garra rufa*. These tiny fish love dead epidermis and leave behind feet as smooth as those of a baby. No word on whether *Garra rufa* enjoy a side of face with their feet.

Q Does eating turkey make you tired?

A Please put your La-Z-Boy into an upright position—you'll want to be awake for this. While the post-Thanksgiving snooze is a widely experienced phenomenon, turkey is not to blame for it.

The game bird got its bum rap because it contains L-tryptophan, the amino acid popularly known for its sleep-inducing effects. When digested, L-tryptophan travels through the bloodstream to the brain. Once there, it's metabolized into the neurotransmitters serotonin and melatonin. These chemical substances have a calming effect on the body and help us get to sleep.

Now you might think the proof is right there on the holiday platter. But the truth is, scientists know that L-tryptophan can really only make you drowsy if taken purely, on an empty stomach, without any other amino acids. As a protein-rich food, turkey just happens to be loaded with other amino acids.

Furthermore, compared to other common foods, turkey does not contain unusually high levels of L-tryptophan. Chicken, pork, cheese, beef, and soybeans have as much—or more—per equivalent portion.

So what gives? How did turkey get its reputation as a sleeping agent? For one, it's often the centerpiece of the traditional Thanksgiving meal—so much so that we might discount all the starchy, sugary carbohydrates and fats (i.e., stuffing, mashed potatoes, gravy, bread, pumpkin pie, and sweet potatoes smothered with marshmallows) that also take their toll.

Nutritionists say it's not the turkey that makes us tired, but the massive overeating. The average person consumes about three thousand calories and 229 grams of fat—well more than a full day's allotment—over the course of a Thanksgiving meal.

It takes a great deal of energy to digest such a large dinner. And when you have a full stomach, blood is directed away from your brain and nervous system and toward your digestive track. The result? Before you know it, your pants are popped and you're feeling sleepy... very sleepy.

Q Does the body really have its own clock?

A It's no crock of New Age malarkey—the body does have an internal clock. Indeed, you don't always eat because your body has run out of fuel, and you don't necessarily sleep because you've used up your energy. A great deal of your behavior is governed by a daily cycle within your body. It's kind of creepy when you think about it—who is in control here? But before you mount a coup against your hypothalamus, learn more about your internal clock.

Your body unconsciously regulates a daily series of processes to help you perform simple functions, such as awakening and remembering to eat. In the early morning hours, for example, your body stops producing melatonin, a neurotransmitter that makes you sleepy, and raises your blood pressure and body temperature in preparation for waking up.

These cycles are not exclusive to humans. All living organisms, including plants, have biological schedules. In some animals, signals from the body can mean the difference between life and death. A nocturnal rodent, for instance, uses the cover of darkness to avoid predators while foraging for food. If that rodent were to suddenly venture out during daylight, it would be at risk from all sorts of creatures.

The fancy name for this internal clock is "circadian rhythm." The term stems from the Latin *circa* ("about") and *dia* ("day") and refers to the twenty-four-hour period during which these processes take place.

As with any good rhythm, it's a poor idea to suddenly change the tempo. Disrupting your circadian rhythm can trigger health problems, including impaired cognitive function, obesity, and even diabetes. Many things can throw your circadian rhythm out of whack, from jet lag to clinical depression. Up all night cramming for a final? If you feel lousy the next day, it's not just because you're tired—you've derailed your body's natural cycle.

So while the body does run its own maintenance schedule without your knowledge or consent, it still needs your cooperation to get the job done. That means going to bed at a decent hour, setting the alarm, and eating a proper breakfast. Our circadian rhythm is more of a partnership than a dictatorship.

Q Why do body parts "fall asleep"?

A It happens to all of us. You get up in the middle of the night because nature is calling, but it's hard to walk because one of your feet is "asleep." As a tingling sensation shoots through your foot, you lumber toward the bathroom like Frankenstein's monster.

What's happening? It begins when a limb has had pressure exerted on it for an extended period of time, maybe from kneeling or from crossing your arms. When this happens, the nerves in the limb obviously have pressure exerted on them, too, and this prevents those nerves from sending messages to the brain and the rest of the body. Blood vessels in the limb are also squeezed, which means oxygen being carried to the nerves is blocked and never makes it. Simply put, in the airport that is your body, too much pressure cancels a lot of incoming and outgoing flights.

The brain isn't sure what's going on—some nerves aren't transmitting any information to it, while others are sending impulses erratically. As a sort of warning signal, the limb starts to tingle. It's your body's way of saying, "Get out of that kneeling position, for crying out loud, before you cause nerve damage."

Once you jostle the affected limb, the nerves begin functioning properly again. Of course, it doesn't happen instantly. The tingling sensation often intensifies and is followed by a somewhat uncomfortable semi-numbness.

Why does this occur? Your nerves comprise bundles of fibers, and each transmits different signals to the brain. The fibers that control touch are among the thickest, and they're the last to "wake up" and resume the proper firing of impulses. That's why the final feeling you have before your limb returns to normal is that odd sensation of semi-numbness, the one that makes you look like you're starring in a B-grade horror flick.

Q What happens when you get the wind knocked out of you?

A "Getting the wind knocked out of you" is what happens when you suffer a blow to the abdomen or back and then have difficultly breathing regularly. Does getting the wind knocked out of you mean that you're a wimp? Nope, it's something that can happen to anyone—even to the toughest NFL football players. It's all about the diaphragm.

The diaphragm is a muscle that extends just below your rib cage and under your lungs; it separates your lungs from your abdominal cavity. When you inhale, your diaphragm contracts downward, which not only makes room for more air in the lungs, but also creates a vacuum to help pull air in. When you exhale, the muscle relaxes upward and helps to push air out. The diaphragm is sort of like the lungs' spotter.

When that bully punches you in the stomach (technically, in the solar plexus), or when a linebacker tackles you and you land hard on your back, your diaphragm may start to spasm. When it's in this state, the diaphragm takes some "me time" to get back into balance and does not move down or up to help the air come and go. Once the spasms cease, your breathing returns to normal. While the diaphragm is stabilizing, you hear the wheezing that is associated with getting the wind knocked out of you.

It doesn't take long—usually only a minute or two—to get your wind back. So stay calm, don't panic, and give it time. If you don't get your wind back after a couple of minutes, then you can panic—and see a doctor.

Q Why do men have an Adam's apple, but women don't?

A An Adam's apple is the protrusion of cartilage around the voice box or larynx. And it's not just a guy thing—all men and women have this anatomical feature, though it's larger and usually much more evident in men. The technical term for this bump in your throat that moves up and down when you talk is the *prominentia laryngea*. So why is it that men have a larger and more obvious *prominentia*... uh, Adam's apple? It goes back—like so many of the important things—to that painful time of life when a boy becomes a man. You know, puberty.

When a boy hits adolescence, his larynx begins to grow. Eventually, this enlarging of the voice box gives him access to the deep tones that characterize the speech of all red-blooded men—but in the meantime, our awkward pubescent hero has to contend with a squeaky, scratchy voice that cracks when he even thinks of asking a girl to dance. And as his larynx grows, the surrounding cartilage builds up and pushes outward, giving rise to the prominent Adam's apple that will soon be covered in countless nicks from his incompetent attempts at shaving.

But it's a different story for girls who are on the verge of womanhood. Typically their larynxes don't get any larger as they mature, sparing them from one of the slighter indignities of puberty. And that is why women don't have (or don't appear to have) an Adam's apple.

But why is it called an Adam's apple in the first place? There are a couple of explanations. Some people believe that the Adam's apple derives its name from the Biblical story of Adam and Eve. As Adam chewed and then began to swallow his first bite of that crisp forbidden fruit, he was so horrified by the wrath of God—or by the fact that his girlfriend suddenly had clothes on—that the fruit got stuck in his throat.

The second theory is less colorful but probably more accurate: It could be a mistranslation from Hebrew. *Tappauch ha adam* means "male bump," but it may have been misunderstood to mean "Adam's apple."

Regardless of what you call it, there will always be some people with an irrational dislike of their own Adam's apples. If you yourself can't stand it, you can get cosmetic surgery to reduce its size. The procedure is called a chondrolaryngoplasty. Say that three times fast . . . unless you've just had a chondrolaryngoplasty. In this case, give your voice a rest.

Q Why do you remember some things and forget other things?

A The short answer: No one knows for sure. Cracking the mystery of memory is among the trickiest games in science. But neurologists do have some thoughts.

Memories are patterns of electrochemical connections between neurons. Neurons are the thinkin' nerve cells in your brain. A standard-issue human brain comes with about one hundred billion neurons, which are connected to one another at points called synapses. When you form a memory, you strengthen existing synapses and create new synapses. This fashions a connection pattern among a big group of neurons.

With so many neurons, there are virtually limitless connection patterns, which means virtually limitless possible thoughts. How these patterns add up to Grandma's casserole recipe or the plot of *Police Academy 4* boggles the mind, but that's the basic idea.

No memory is an island, however. Anything you remember is connected to other things you remember, stored as neuron-connection patterns in various places. For example, when you remember winning the big break-dancing contest, the dancing part could be in one part of the brain, the music part in another. And both could be connected to other memories of your hip-hop career, which are scattered all over the brain.

The more that memories are connected to other memories, the greater the likelihood that those memories will "stick." You're more apt to remember details of meeting your spouse than meeting your dry cleaner. The spouse-meeting memories connect to all kinds of other things that you remember about your spouse. The dry cleaner memories connect to a few basically identical trips to the dry cleaner. The spouse-meeting is also an emotional memory, which makes it especially well-connected in the world of neurons. In simple terms, you're more likely to stumble across a memory if it's connected to a number of memories, and if those memories involve emotion.

And the more frequently you recall something, the more likely you are to remember it. Whenever you remember something, you essentially create a new memory—a brand new version of the event that is based on your new thoughts about it. This establishes new connections, which makes it easier to recall the memory. For example, if you dial the same phone number often enough, eventually you'll memorize it because it's scrawled all over your brain.

New information is more likely to stick in your memory if it connects to information you already know. You'll remember directions to a new spot in your hometown more readily than directions in a foreign city because you already know many streets and neighborhoods in your hometown.

Paying close attention also helps, of course. When committing something to memory, your brain automatically filters out what it perceives as extraneous information. This helps keep us sane: Imagine living with the memory of every overheard checkout-line conversation buzzing in your head. But this automatic filter may also make you forget where you put your keys if you were freestyle rappin' when you set them down.

What was the question again?

Q Why do we sweat?

A Human sweat glands are like a built-in sprinkler system. Sweat enables us to cool off when the exterior temperature rises (due to changes in the weather) or when our interior temperatures rise (due to exercise, anxiety, or illness). Sweat is one of the mechanisms that our bodies use to keep us at a steady—and healthy—98.6 degrees Fahrenheit.

Here are the basics: Humans have about 2.6 million sweat glands, but not all of these glands produce the same kind of sweat. Sweat has two distinct sources: eccrine and apocrine glands. Eccrine glands exist all over the body and are active from birth. They constantly release a salty, nearly odorless fluid onto the skin, though you probably only notice this sweat when it's really hot or you've been working out really hard. Apocrine glands, on the other hand, are concentrated in the armpits, on the soles of the feet, in the palms of the hands, and in the groin. They become active during puberty. Yes, puberty and perspiration go hand in hand.

Apocrine glands don't secrete liquid directly onto the skin. Instead, each gland empties into a hair follicle. When a person is under emotional or physical stress, the tiny muscle around the hair follicle contracts, pushing the liquid onto the skin, where it becomes sweat. Apocrine glands carry lipids and proteins, as well as water and salt. When these substances mix with the sebaceous oils in the hair follicles and then meet the bacteria on the skin, well, that's when you begin to hold your nose.

But before you start thinking of eccrine as "good" sweat and apocrine as "bad," consider this: Apocrine sweat has been found to contain androsterone pheromones, those mysterious musky odors that are responsible for sexual arousal. So sweat can be sexy, too. Just don't take this as an excuse to wear unwashed gym socks on a date—a few pheromones go a long way.

To banish body odor, a little dab of deodorant should do. Deodorants are based on mildly acidic compounds that dry the skin before the odor starts. Antiperspirants, another popular option, actually block sweat with aluminum salts. Some people think that these salts may be unhealthy, but so far, clinical evidence has failed to connect them to any disease.

If you feel that you sweat too much, or too little, see your doctor. Excessive sweating, officially known as *hyperhidrosis,* and lack of sweat, called *anhidrosis,* are genuine medical conditions with serious complications. Fortunately, both are treatable. For most of us, however-er, dealing with sweat is fairly simple: Take a shower and wear loose and absorbent clothing. For goodness sake, don't sweat about sweat!

Q What is face-blindness?

A Some people never forget a face. Others can't seem to remember one. We see faces everywhere. Sociologists estimate that an adult who lives in a busy urban area encounters more than a thousand different faces every day. For most of us, picking our friends and loved ones out of a crowd is a snap. Homing in on the faces we know is simply an instinct.

But what if you couldn't recognize faces? Not even the ones that belong to the people you know best? If you seem to spend a lot of time apologizing to your nearest and dearest—saying things like, "Sorry, I didn't see you there yesterday. Did you get a new haircut? Were you wearing a different shirt? A pair of Groucho glasses?"—you might be face-blind.

No, you don't need a new pair of contacts. Face-blind people can have 20/20 vision. And chances are, there's nothing wrong with your memory either. You can be a whiz at Trivial Pursuit, a walking encyclopedia of arcane information, and still not be able to recall the face you see across the breakfast table every morning.

Why? Many scientists believe facial recognition is a highly specialized neurological task. It takes place in an area of the brain known as the *fusiform gyrus,* which is located behind your right ear. People who suffer an injury to this part of their brains are likely to have *prosopagnosia,* a fancy medical term for face-blindness. Others seem to be born that way.

Of course, everybody has occasional problems recognizing faces. For the truly face-blind, however, faces may appear only as a blur or a jumble of features that never quite coalesce into the whole that becomes Bill from accounting or Judy from your softball team.

How many people suffer from face-blindness? Statistics are difficult to come by, simply because many people are not even aware that the inability to recognize faces is a bona fide medical syndrome. However, recent research on random samples of college students indicates that *prosopagnosia* may affect as many as one out of every fifty people, or approximately 2 percent of the population.

What can you do if you think that you are face-blind? Most people with *prosopagnosia* compensate without even knowing it. They unconsciously learn to distinguish people by the way they walk or talk, or perhaps by a distinctive hairdo or article of dress. Many face-blind people write down the information to remind themselves later. Some people who suffer from this affliction compare it to being tone deaf or colorblind—an inconvenient but hardly a life-threatening disability.

As with just about anything, a sense of humor helps, too. Ask your friend to warn you before she frosts her hair or he discards that Pearl Jam T-shirt he's proudly worn since you met in, oh, 1996. And if you really want to make sure that you see your friends and family in a crowd, tell them to wear something that you'll be sure to remember. Maybe the Groucho glasses. They work like a charm every time.

Q Why do I see stars when I squeeze shut my eyes or cough with my eyes closed?

A Try this experiment: Close your eyes and point both of the suckers to the right. Then take a finger and gently poke the left side of your left eye. You should see something, usually a vague circle of light.

This "light" isn't really a light—it's called a phosphene. The nerves that have to do with sight can be affected in numerous ways and can fool your brain into thinking that you are seeing light. Inside your eyeballs, there's a gel that can stimulate the retina. The brain gets a message from the retina and thinks, "We must be seeing light," and so you get the fireworks.

As you found out in the little experiment we outlined in the first paragraph, creating pressure on the eye is an effective way to make this happen. Coughing or sneezing puts pressure on the optic nerves, which is why you often see sparks when doing either with your eyes closed. Sneezing, by the way, creates enough pressure to shoot air and debris out at one hundred miles per hour. In addition to making a mess, that kind of pressure can easily affect the retina.

As you get older, these sorts of occurrences sometimes can become more common. In some people, the eye gel starts to pull away from the back of the eye or shrink from the retina. It's called vitreous detachment, and even though it sounds pretty gross, it's not a particularly serious development. Retinal detachment, on the other hand, is quite serious—it occurs when the retina peels away from its support tissue. If you're seeing more and more lights for longer periods, it's probably a good idea to have your eyes checked.

There's another visual phenomenon that isn't exactly a phosphene. It's called a floater. Sometimes you see floaters when you're staring at the sky, and it happens more often as you get older. They're visible clumps of eye gel that look like shadows or threads that float across your eye. They're pretty freaky, but fear not—they pass in only a few seconds.

Q Why do some people dream in black and white?

A There's an old saying that nothing is less interesting than another person's dream—unless you are in it. Yet the mystery of dreams has fascinated philosophers and scientists for thousands of years. Aristotle wrote an entire treatise on the subject in 350 BC. Much later, around the dawn of the twentieth century, Sigmund Freud developed an elaborate system of dream interpretation that mostly involved sex.

For all the research that has been done on dream phenomena, surprisingly little has been learned about the function of dreaming. And outside of color symbolists and New Age dream interpreters, few researchers have worked in the area of colors in dreams. But according to studies conducted in the past several years, anywhere from 12 to 20 percent of people dream in black and white.

Several theories have been put forth to explain the drab dream worlds of those 12 to 20 percent. The first of these—corroborated by a number of different dream researchers, including Harvard's J. Allan Hobson, a pioneer on the subject—points to the ephemeral nature of dreams. Everyone has had the experience of waking up from a really cool dream, only to have the details of the plot fade away even as you are trying to confusedly relate them to your bored spouse or roommate at the breakfast table. In the same way, this research suggests, everyone dreams in color, but the memory of the colors fades as quickly as the details do. Most people forget their dreams as soon as they awaken or gradually over the course of a day. But this does not explain why a small percentage of the population reports dreaming in black and white.

Other researchers take a more Jungian tack, suggesting that colors, like the events and objects in dreams, are symbols of the subconscious. Different colors symbolize different emotions—red is passion and drive, blue is calmness and rest, etc.—and shades of gray symbolize a desire to shield oneself from subconscious messages. For example, a red truck in a dream might symbolize passionate assertiveness, while a gray truck might indicate a desire to mask that assertiveness.

Perhaps the most interesting theory about color in dreams was proposed by University of California–Berkeley psychologist Eric Schwitzgebel in a 2002 paper, "Why Did We Think We Dreamed in Black and White?" Schwitzgebel looked at the history of dream research and noticed that the percentage of people who reported colored dreams began to plummet in the late nineteenth century, reached a low of about 30 percent in the late 1950s, and spiked back up as the twentieth century progressed.

Were people really that dull in the first half of the twentieth century? Perhaps. But Schwitzgebel points to something else: The popular forms of media during that period (photography, movies, television) were in black and white. Prior to the invention of photography, black-and-white coloring was rare. (Have you ever seen a classical painting in black and white?) But with the advent of black-and-white photography, many people thought of images—especially everyday images—as being in black and white.

With the rise of film and television, the phenomenon increased. Many of us think of our dreams as movies anyway, and it would be natural for people who had been exposed only to black-and-white film and photography to remember their dreams as drained of color.

If Schwitzgebel's theory is true, one wonders what the future trend might be. Perhaps everyone will start dreaming in CGI.

Q Why is yawning contagious?

A You may think we yawn because we're tired or bored, or because oxygen levels in our lungs are low (that's the traditional medical explanation, after all). But did you know that babies yawn in utero? (They pick up the habit as early as eleven weeks after conception.) Fetuses don't take in oxygen through their lungs, and there's no way they are tired or bored— they sleep all day, and they certainly haven't viewed enough television to have problems with attention span.

Olympic athletes have been known to yawn right before competing in events. Yawning also has been connected to certain conditions, including multiple sclerosis and penile erection (and you just thought your boyfriend was drowsy). Weird, huh?

Scientists don't fully understand why we yawn. Does involuntarily opening one's mouth wide serve any useful or healthful purpose? It's something of a mystery. We do know, however, that 55 percent of people will yawn within five minutes of seeing someone else do it. It's a phenomenon called "contagious yawning." Sometimes just hearing, thinking, or reading

about a yawn is enough to make you unconsciously follow suit. (Did it work?) Again, scientists don't know exactly why, though they have paid it enough mind to conjure a few theories.

Some researchers hypothesize that contagious yawning is more common among the empathetic crowd. In other words, those of us who demonstrate a greater ability to understand and share other people's feelings are more likely to emulate their yawns.

Taking that theory one step further, Dr. Gordon Gallup and researchers at the University of Albany say that empathetic or contagious yawning evolved as a way to "maintain group vigilance." Gallup thinks yawning keeps our brains working at cool, efficient, and alert levels. So in the days of early man, contagious yawning helped raise the attentiveness and danger-detecting abilities of the whole group.

Even today, members of paratrooper regiments and airborne units report yawning together right before a jump. Could contagious yawning really be leftover hardwiring from the days of yore? Quite possibly. Other theories contend that contagious yawning may have been a more explicit form of early communication. The "herding theory" suggests humans might have used contagious yawning to coordinate their behavior. One member of the group would yawn to signal an event, as if to say, "Hey, let's to go hunt for a saber tooth tiger." And the other members in the group would yawn back to reply, "Yeah, let's go."

Humans aren't the only creatures that yawn. Foxes, sea lions, hippos, dogs, and cats are among the animals that do it. Recent studies have even demonstrated that some animals, like dogs and chimpanzees, may suffer from contagious yawning.

Q Can you serve in the U.S. military if you have flat feet?

A It may sound like an urban legend started by draft dodgers, but it isn't. If you have *pes planus* (flat feet), you can't serve in the U.S. military.

Pes planus is a condition in which the longitudinal arch in the foot, which runs from the heel to the ball, has flattened out or never developed normally. The condition can be genetic. It also can result from a malady such as diabetes, a stroke, rheumatoid arthritis, or a foot injury. Even though many people who have flat feet rarely have symptoms or problems beyond foot pain, the U.S. military does not want anything to do with an archless individual.

Documentation on the subject from the U.S. Army, issued December 14, 2007, states: "Current symptomatic *pes planus* (acquired (734) or congenital (754.6)) or history of *pes planus* corrected by prescription or custom orthotics is disqualifying." Translation: Even if your flat feet are under control with shoe inserts, you still can't be all that you can be.

Other foot-related maladies that prevent one from joining the U.S. military are hammer toes, overriding toes, club foot, ingrown toenails, and/or toe deformities. Why? Easy. These conditions may prevent a soldier from wearing military footwear properly, thus impairing walking, running, marching, and jumping. The U.S. armed forces has no room for, "Hup, two, three, *ouch!*"

Chapter Two

ANIMAL KINGDOM

Q Is sex painful for porcupines?

A You've probably heard the old joke: How do porcupines mate? Answer: Very carefully. *(Groan.)*

Okay, okay, the joke was probably funnier the first time around, when it was uttered by one of our ancestors in a caveman comedy club at the dawn of time—but the question remains. With those prickly barbs covering their bodies, how in the name of Saint Raphael do porcupines get it on?

The distinct possibility of taking a quill to the crotch in the line of duty is actually just the tip of the iceberg—the mating ritual of the porcupine is fraught with even more frustration, danger, and oddity than you might expect. The porcupine's sex habits are as strange as the most bizarre sexual practices of humans (not that we'd know anything about those).

For starters, there's only one brief window each year when a porcupine can get lucky: a mating season that occurs in late fall and lasts about a month. Even during that one time of the year when those prickly hormones are raging, a female porcupine is sexually receptive for only eight to twelve hours. And when the female isn't in the mood, there's no way to persuade her—her quills act as a natural defense mechanism that is painfully effective.

When the female porcupine is ready to mate, she lets the men know by calling to them. She then scrambles into the nearest tree and waits for her suitors to arrive. And arrive they do. Male porcupines that have been suffering for nearly an entire year sprint to the clarion call of sweet, sweet relief. But before they can take part in the gentle act of love, there is a period of courtship.

The amorous male scampers up the tree with his beloved, then demonstrates his passion for her the only way he knows how: by blasting the object of his affection with a powerful stream of urine. The young couple remains together in the tree for a few days, during which time the male periodically super soaks the female with intense streams of urine that can travel up to six feet. (Naturalists don't entirely understand the porcupine's affection for water sports, though they hypothesize that hormones in the male's urine help the female "get in the mood.")

It's not all romance and pee for the courting male. Before gaining access, he must pass another test. (No, it's not producing a bank statement.) When other male porcupines show up looking for love, our hero must defend his urine-soaked lover, taking on challengers and fighting them—sometimes to the death—for the right to couple with the female porcupine.

Finally, after a successful courtship, the time comes for the porcupines to consummate their love. The female curls her tail over her back and offers her quill-less backside to the male. The male approaches—*very carefully*—and at long last mounts his mate. The male's underside is also without quills, making the actual act of coupling relatively painless.

As one would expect of an animal that's gone nearly a year without sex, the male doesn't perform exceedingly well. The intercourse lasts only five or six seconds. This should make the men reading this feel much better about themselves, even as it must sorely disappoint the female porcupine, which has put up with quite a lot for such a brief performance.

Q Do woodpeckers get headaches?

A Oh, the lengths that the earth's inhabitants will go for a little love and affection. Manakin birds perform elaborate dance routines that resemble early Michael Jackson more than anything ornithological. Hippos attract their mates by defecating all over the place. Humans seek attention from the opposite sex by putting smelly chemicals on their skin, and installing sweet neon lights around their license plates. But to the lovelorn of all species, the woodpecker's efforts may seem the most fitting:

During mating season, male woodpeckers bang their heads against any available hard surface up to twelve thousand times a day.

Though metaphorically apt, it seems that this head-banging ritual would be awfully painful. And it leads us to wonder whether woodpeckers get headaches. Fortunately, Philip May, a neuro-psychiatrist at the University of California, spent a good deal of time studying this subject. And though he didn't definitively answer the question of whether woodpeckers get headaches—after all, it's impossible to ask a wood-pecker how its head feels—he did figure out why woodpeckers are able to bash their faces against trees all day (with the equivalent force of running into a wall face-first at sixteen miles per hour) without turning into pulp.

According to a 2002 *British Journal of Ophthalmology* article summarizing May's findings, the woodpecker is blessed with an anatomy particularly well suited to head-banging. The woodpeck-er's skull, for example, is proportionally thicker than your average animal cranium. At the same time, its brain is housed in a skull that's virtually devoid of the cranial fluid that humans have. So while a few blows to the noggin will send the human brain swim-ming, the woodpecker's sits firmly in place.

Woodpeckers also have special musculature along the jaw and neck that act as shock absorbers, and a nictitating mem-brane—also known as a third eyelid—that closes every time the bird hammers against a tree, preventing eye injuries. Finally, the woodpecker's uncanny geometric ability to strike wood at a perfectly perpendicular angle helps disperse force equally throughout the head and body.

Of course, the woodpecker's anatomy is both a blessing and a curse. While its makeup may help it lure a mate, it will never be able to use the excuse that has helped countless males and females: "Not tonight, honey—I have a headache."

Q Why are skunks so stinky?

A Oh, so you smell like a bed of roses? But seriously, skunks have earned their odiferous reputation through their marvelous ability to make other things stink to high heaven.

All eleven species of skunk have stinky spray housed in their anal glands. However, as dog owners can attest, skunks aren't the only animals to have anal glands filled with terrible-smelling substances. Opossums are particularly bad stinkers; an opossum will empty its anal glands when "playing dead" to help it smell like a rotting corpse. While no animal's anal glands are remotely fragrant, skunks' pack an especially pungent stench. This is because skunks use their spray as a defense mechanism. And they have amazing range: Skunks have strong muscles surrounding the glands, which allow them to spray sixteen feet or more on a good day.

A skunk doesn't want to stink up the place. It does everything in its power to warn predators before it douses its target with *eau de skunk*. A skunk will jump up and down, stomp its feet, hiss, and lift its tail in the air, all in the hope that the predator will realize that it's dealing with a skunk and go away. A skunk only does what it does best when it feels it has no choice. Then it releases the nauseating mix of thiols (chemicals that contain super-stinky sulfur), which makes whatever it hits undateable for the foreseeable future. Skunks have enough "stink juice" stored up for about five or six sprays; after they empty their anal glands, it takes up to ten days to replenish the supply.

Being sprayed by a skunk is an extremely unpleasant experience. Besides the smell, the spray from a skunk can cause nausea and temporary blindness. Bobcats, foxes, coyotes, and badgers usually only hunt skunk if they are really, really hungry. Only the great horned owl makes skunk a regular snack—and the fact that the great horned owl barely has a sense of smell probably has a lot to do with it.

Should you find yourself on the receiving end of a skunk shower, your best deodorizer is alkaline hydrogen peroxide. But unless you startle a skunk (which is possible, since the critter doesn't have keen eyesight), you'll probably have plenty of chances not to get sprayed. You and a skunk have a lot in common: You don't want to get sprayed, and the skunk doesn't want to spray you.

Q How do carrier pigeons know where to go?

A No family vacation would be complete without at least one episode of Dad grimly staring straight ahead, gripping the steering wheel and declaring that he is not lost as Mom insists on stopping for directions. Meanwhile, the kids are tired, night is falling, and nobody's eaten anything except a handful of Cheetos for the past six hours. But Dad is not lost. He will not stop.

It's well known that men believe they have some sort of innate directional ability—and why not? If a creature as dull and dim-witted as a carrier pigeon can find its way home without any maps or directions from gas-station attendants, a healthy human male should certainly be able to do the same.

Little does Dad know that the carrier pigeon has a secret weapon. It's called magnetite, and its recent discovery in the beaks of carrier pigeons may help solve the centuries-old mystery of just how carrier pigeons know their way home.

Since the fifth century BC, when they were used for communication between Syria and Persia, carrier pigeons have been prized for their ability to find their way home, sometimes over distances of more than five hundred miles. In World War I and World War II, Allied forces made heavy use of carrier pigeons, sending messages with them from base to base to avoid having radio signals intercepted or if the terrain prevented a clear signal. In fact, several carrier pigeons were honored with war medals.

For a long time, there was no solid evidence to explain how these birds were able to find their way anywhere, despite theories that ranged from an uncanny astronomical sense to a heightened olfactory ability to an exceptional sense of hearing. Recently, though, scientists made an important discovery: bits of magnetic crystal, called magnetite, embedded in the beaks of carrier pigeons. This has led some researchers to believe that carrier pigeons have magneto reception—the ability to detect changes in the earth's magnetic fields—which is a sort of built-in compass that guides these birds to their destinations.

Scientists verified the important role of magnetite through a study that examined the effects of magnetic fields on the birds' homing ability. When the scientists blocked the birds' magnetic ability by attaching small magnets to their beaks, the pigeons' ability to orient themselves plummeted by almost 50 percent. There was no report, however, on whether this handicap stopped male pigeons from plunging blindly forward. We'd guess not.

Q Do you have a better chance against an alligator or a crocodile?

A The conditions are the key here. If either you or the animal is caught unaware, the advantage likely goes to the beast. Animals in the wild have instincts and reflexes honed by their survival-of-the-fittest lifestyles; our instincts and reflexes have been dulled by years of channel surfing.

But if you enter into a staged setting with an alligator or a crocodile and do battle *mano a garra,* your chances are much improved. Alligator and crocodile wrestling has been a common sideshow attraction in the U.S. for at least fifty years. While these showbiz animals are more accustomed to being around people, and are thus less vicious than gators and crocs that have never had any human contact, there is risk involved. Wrestlers are bitten all the time. Still, they wouldn't enter the ring if they didn't think they could maintain the upper hand.

According to professional crocodile and alligator wrestlers, both animals can be unpredictable. And when they get their jaws around one of your limbs, you're pretty much toast. Even famed croc wrangler Steve "Crocodile Hunter" Irwin said that if he felt a death roll coming on, he backed off from the animal.

Your chances of survival depend largely upon the size of the animal, and here is where we'll declare the winner of this debate. The saltwater crocodile is the largest living reptile species in terms of mass; it's known to grow as long as twenty feet, and it carries the reputation of being the most aggressive of the crocodilian species. In just ten years, between 1980 and 1990, the saltwater crocodile killed eight people in Australia.

Meanwhile, the American alligator averages around fifteen feet in length. In a fifty-eight-year period (1948 to 2006), the American alligator killed nineteen people in Florida and Georgia; of the reported alligator attacks in Texas, South Carolina, Alabama, and Louisiana in the same time period, none resulted in death.

The bigger and stronger animal is more difficult to keep under control, and if it gets the upper hand, it has a better chance of ripping you to shreds. The saltwater crocodile, given its greater size and meaner mind-set, is more inclined to do both.

So if you must choose one, you probably have a better chance against the alligator. That's on land, of course. In the water, your chances of survival are slim to none, regardless of the animal you're up against. Alligators and crocodiles are known to take out animals much larger than themselves while in the water—cows, buffalo, and even hippos. Your best bet is to stay safely on the couch, with your beloved remote control firmly in hand.

Q Can chickens fly?

A Anyone who has watched a chicken attempt to fly can't help but feel sorry for the little creature. It's a combination of a hop, a lunge, and a spasm, so calling what a chicken does "flying" is more than a slight exaggeration.

Why can't chickens fly? After all, they're birds, which means that they have wings. Why not spread those wings and follow their feathered brothers and sisters into the sky?

The problem is that because it's bred to provide humans with jumbo eggs, meaty thighs, and voluptuous breasts, the domestic chicken just isn't very aerodynamic. Furthermore, most domestic chickens are raised in cages on poultry farms and have scarcely enough room to move, let alone fly.

Chickens weren't always grounded. Though they would never have been confused with soaring eagles, chickens did fly at one time in their evolutionary history. The wild red jungle fowl of India, from which chickens are descended, is still able to flap its way up to the tops of trees to escape predators. But for today's domestic chickens, flight is just a distant memory stored deep within their genetic makeup. Besides, these dim-witted animals are far more interested in what's on the ground (seed) than what's above them (sky).

There are a few breeds of chicken that you may still spot in trees or on the tops of fence posts, such as bantams or other smaller varieties. Free-range chickens, which get to run around the farmer's barnyard instead of growing fat and lazy on a roost all day, can also approximate flight—which is the reason that many have their wings clipped. We suspect that these clipped free-rangers aren't the chickens you'll be chowing down during your neighborhood bar's next ten-cent wing night.

Q Can my pet goldfish lower my blood pressure?

A If you have an aquarium, you probably already realize that watching fish swim around is pretty calming. In fact, research shows that even a small aquarium can help reduce stress, at least temporarily. That's why there are fish tanks in the waiting rooms of many doctors' and dentists' offices.

In the 1980s, researchers at the University of Pennsylvania found that watching fish in an aquarium is far more effective at reducing stress than watching an aquarium without fish. In 1999, Nancy Edwards, a professor of nursing at Purdue University, discovered that Alzheimer's patients who were exposed to fish-filled aquariums were more relaxed and alert, and that they even began to eat a healthier diet. Another study showed that exposure to aquariums can contribute to decreased stress and hyperactivity among patients with Attention Deficit Hyperactivity Disorder.

Nobody is sure exactly why fish are so calming. The Purdue University study theorized that the combination of movement, color, and sound in an aquarium has a relaxing effect.

But it's not just fish that help reduce stress. Having a pet of any kind leads to better health. A 2007 study at Queen's University in Belfast, Northern Ireland, showed that dog owners tended to have lower blood pressure and cholesterol than non-dog owners. The study proposed that pet owners in general are healthier than the population on average and also suggested that having a dog is better for you than having a cat. However, the study didn't weigh in on how dogs and cats compare to fish.

If you don't fancy keeping an aquarium, you can always just *eat* fish. Most fish contain a bunch of omega 3 fatty acids that are good for your heart and blood pressure. However, if you're thinking of swallowing Goldie for these fatty acids, think again. Though goldfish are members of the carp family, and carp are oily fish (which means they've got a lot of essential fatty acids), goldfish require just the right diet to create these fatty acids.

Q Cows are in herds, and fish are in schools. What about other animals?

A Ever heard of a sloth of bears? How about an unkindness of ravens?

There's an almost endless array of collective nouns for animals, people, and objects. Many of them—and many of the most interesting—come from *The Book of St. Albans,* published in 1486. The book includes a long list of collective nouns for groups of animals; most were meant to be used by hunters in the field.

Some group names describe attributes we ascribe to the animals. For example, a parliament of owls reflects the notion that owls are wise. An ambush describes a group of tigers, reflecting their predatory tactics. What do you call a group of apes, those regal mammals known for their superior intellect? A shrewdness, of course. Some terms stem from physical characteristics, like a prickle of porcupines or a tower of giraffes. Others are just plain poetic: a murder of crows.

Some collective nouns are used for multiple species. You can have a pod of dolphins, whales, or seals. You can have a flock of birds or, get this, a flock of camels. Some animals are described by more than one collective noun. You can have a storytelling of ravens or an unkindness of ravens.

The names can be highly specific. A group of geese on the ground is a gaggle; flying, it's a skein; flying in a V formation, you've got yourself a wedge.

Collective nouns don't just apply to animals. They can describe objects and people, too. There's a flood of tears, a quiver of arrows, a range of mountains. And if one isn't enough, you can call upon a host of angels, a slate of candidates, or a sentence of judges.

Why not create your own collective descriptions? Gather a lead of pencils and a tree of papers, and get to work.

Q Do animals get high?

A Have you ever watched cats go nuts over catnip? Or cattle graze on locoweed? Or bighorn sheep chew on psychedelic lichen growing on rocks? If so, you know that animals do indeed get high.

In fact, we humans have been known to follow animals down the state-altering trail. Coffee was just red berries on a shrub until the Assyrians noticed that their goats were incredibly energized by eating them. Peruvian legend holds that pumas discovered medicinal quinine; sick pumas would eat the bark of the cinchona tree, and the quinine juice would heal them. The Tukano Indians of South America say that jaguars, which are normally strict carnivores, eat the bark of the yaje vine and have hallucinations; some Tukanos have tried it themselves, wanting to develop "jaguar eyes."

Animals can become addicted to intoxicants, which actually has helped humans treat their own addictions. Paul Czoty, a researcher from Wake Forest University, has experimented with encouraging addiction to cocaine in monkeys and then treating it with amphetamines. Czoty is confident that his research will be used in developing treatment programs for human cocaine addiction. Researchers also have used animals to help treat human addiction to alcohol, tobacco, and other substances.

UCLA psycho-pharmaceutical researcher Ronald K. Siegel calls the pursuit of intoxication for both humans and animals "the fourth drive," something that is as deeply felt as the need for food, water, and sex. Remember that the next time you see your cat rolling around in a daze after getting into some catnip.

Q Do animals have orgasms?

A Research into human sexuality is fraught with controversy, so imagine the arguments regarding animal sexuality. There is, however, one point on which all zoologists would agree: Male animals have orgasms. Without such orgasms, species would not survive. Whether the male animal enjoys himself is a different matter. Consider the poor salmon that swim long distances upstream in order to ejaculate. Or consider any of the cannibalistic arachnids, such as the *Argiope aurantia* (also called the black-and-yellow garden spider): The male of the species spontaneously dies during sex.

A more controversial matter is whether female animals have orgasms. Certainly, females in many species are receptive to sex when they are fertile. Zoologists used to think that females were motivated solely by a desire to reproduce; now, they believe that there has to be a more immediate reward at stake than the promise of offspring. All female mammals have clitorises and, therefore, the theoretical capacity to have an orgasm.

While most mammalian sexual encounters are brief and seem to be focused exclusively on male ejaculation, higher-order primates, such as bonobos, seem to take more time going at it. Female mammals of the higher, smarter orders—for example, dolphins, monkeys, and gorillas—have discovered ways other than intercourse to bring about orgasm, much like humans have. Some zoologists have observed female mammals stimulating themselves or being stimulated in a manner that would suggest pleasure-seeking. Experiments with rhesus monkeys and chimps in which the clitoris has been stimulated have resulted in uterine contractions that might mean orgasm. Even the not-so-bright cow has been stimulated to such contractions.

Zoologists and human sexologists argue about whether female orgasms have an evolutionary function—do they help the vitality of the species? Some sexologists argue that female orgasms are a means of selecting a mate who is more likely to be a good father: a male who takes his time and is deliberate about pleasuring his mate is more likely to exhibit qualities of patience, loyalty, and attentiveness that might be absent in a typical alpha male. Therefore, a female's desire for an orgasm, and her choice of a mate with whom she has this experience, leads to better odds for conception and a better survival rate among the offspring.

On the other side of the argument, biologist and science philosopher Elizabeth Lloyd contends in her book *The Case of the Female Orgasm: Bias in the Science of Evolution* that female orgasms serve no biological function and that the presence of the clitoris in a primate is vestigial, like nipples on the male chest. In Lloyd's view, both the clitoris and nipples are merely products of being developmentally linked to the opposite sex.

In any event, until we can be like Dr. Doolittle and talk to the animals, the answer to this question will remain an educated guess.

Q Does a two-hump camel store more water than a one-hump camel?

A First, let's give the poor beasts their proper names. A two-hump camel is called a Bactrian camel and comes from the plains of Asia. A one-hump camel is the most commonly known to Westerners; it's called a dromedary camel, and it hails from the Middle East and Africa.

Okay then, which one stores more water in its hump(s)? Um, it's actually neither, despite what your teachers may have told you. What camels actually store in there is good old fat. That's right, the camel's hump is a bit like our beer belly, except the hump is far more efficient and useful.

The hump doesn't have much to do with water conservation. It's there to provide the camel with nourishment when it has no food. If the camel uses up all the fat in its hump, the empty hump will droop until the animal gets more food. (That's why malnourished camels often have droopy humps.) Camels can go for several weeks without food due to their humps—the bigger its hump, the longer a camel can go without food.

So the humps have got food covered, but what about water? We can't escape the fact that camels sometimes go days without water as well as food. Luckily, camels are really good at conserving water. When they have access to water, they drink between twenty and thirty gallons in about ten minutes—they can drink forty-five gallons in twenty-four hours. This water is then stored in their blood cells for later use.

Everything about the camel is designed so that it uses as little water as possible. It can withstand significant body temperature changes without needing to perspire; in fact, a camel can go from about 93 degrees to 107 degrees Fahrenheit without breaking a sweat. (If a human being's temperature goes up by two degrees, it indicates illness.) A camel's excretions are even very low in water.

So, does a two-hump camel store more *fat* than a one-hump camel? Yes, but the two animals are designed in such ways that the overall efficiency of the fatty-hump system is probably about the same on both.

Q How do sniffer dogs know what to sniff?

A The same way musicians get to Carnegie Hall: practice, practice, and more practice.

From bloodhounds to bulldogs to Heinz 57s, almost any dog can be trained to follow scents. Doggie noses have twenty to forty times as many nasal receptors as human snouts, which makes them more sensitive than the best man-made instruments. With the right training, dogs can learn to pick out faint traces of any scent—from the types of plastics used in DVDs to bugs or drugs. They may even be able to smell cancer and other diseases.

No matter what odor a dog is being trained to search for, the process is the same: Dogs are given varied items to smell; when they sniff the target odor, they get a reward.

Want a dog to sniff out polycarbonate plastic so that it can find shipments of pirated DVDs at the airport? Several times a day for months, present the dog with a dozen or so choices. You might show it a bologna sandwich, a pen, a wallet, a stuffed animal, and finally a DVD—then give Fido a treat when it takes a whiff of the DVD.

After a few months, the dog associates the odor with praise and treats, and will go after it with passion. As a result of this kind of training, dogs learned how to search for bodies (either alive or dead), stolen money, drugs such as cocaine and marijuana, guns, explosives, land mines, termites, bedbugs, and even toxic mold. The latter takes the most intense training because there are different types of toxic mold that a good search dog must be able to zero in on.

Trained, certified canine sniffers are so sensitive that the U.S. courts recognize them as "scientific instruments." After becoming certified search dogs, canines must train for up to fifty hours a month to maintain their top form. Since the training involves doing what the dog loves to do anyway, training is more of a game than work—at least for the dog.

Toxic mold specialist Rick Koenig of Hermosa Beach, California, uses his sniffer pooch, Savannah, to detect mold in buildings. When he walked his dog into a large, multistory office building one day, the company's vice president was skeptical that a canine could do the job. The vice president laughed out loud when Savannah stopped and indicated that there was mold in a concrete filing unit on the ground floor of the building. The unit was waterproof, fireproof, leakproof—it was everything-proof. How could mold exist there? The unit was opened, and the gooey, moldy remains of a sandwich, hidden behind some files months before, vindicated Savannah. The VP became the dog's biggest champion.

Praise, treats, and a job well done—it's all in a day's work for a sniffer dog.

Q How long would it take a pack of piranhas to polish off a cow?

A The answer to this question hinges on a few factors: How large is the cow? More important, how many fish are there, and how hungry are they? Like sharks, piranhas are drawn to blood; they're killers from the moment they are born. And it's true—a pack of piranhas can indeed strip the flesh from a much larger animal, such as a cow.

The estimated time it would take a school of piranhas to skeletonize a cow varies. Some sources claim less than a minute; others say up to five minutes. But marine biologists call these estimates exaggerations. The piranha has a fearsome, tooth-filled grin—but under normal circumstances, it is not considered overly aggressive.

In the United States, the legend of the ravenous piranha began with Theodore Roosevelt's 1913 trip to South America. He returned full of stories, many of which concerned the carnivorous fish. It is thought that the Brazilian tour guides who were charged with showing President Roosevelt a good time had a joke at his expense by making piranhas out to be more dangerous than they are. There was an incident in which a cow was lowered into a branch of the Rio Aripuana that was teeming with piranhas, and the outcome was every bit as grisly as legend says. But some vital facts were left out of the story. For one, the cow was sick and bleeding, which spurred the fish into a frenzy. Furthermore, the piranhas were isolated, hungry, and ornery.

They saw a meal and went nuts—and we've been talking about it ever since.

Modern jungle-dwellers don't typically see piranhas as a danger. The fish usually feed on small animals—other fish, frogs, and baby caimans. It's not uncommon for a human to be bitten by a piranha, but these wounds are usually small and singular. Little flesh lost, little harm done—the fish and the human go their separate ways.

Of course, this isn't to say that piranhas lack the capacity to wreak havoc. Piranhas are known to be most vicious during the dry season. They are believed to travel in large schools for the purpose of protection, and they stimulate one another at feeding time. In light of this information, there are instances when you don't want to get anywhere near a piranha. If you have an open wound, for instance, it might be a good idea to forego that afternoon dip in the Rio Aripuana.

Q If bats are blind, how do they know where they're going?

A We've all heard the expression "blind as a bat"—but the fact is, bats can see. All bat species have eyes, and some have pretty good vision.

Take the Megachiroptera bat (more commonly known as the Old World fruit bat or flying fox). Members of this tropical suborder are known for their large eyes and excellent nighttime eyesight. Studies have shown that they're able to see things at lower light levels than even humans can. Most Megachiroptera bats rely completely on their vision to find the fruits and flower nectar they like to munch while flying around at night.

Smaller Microchiroptera bats count on their eyesight, too. These insect-eating bats can see obstacles and motion while navigating speedy, long-distance trips. However, like many bat species, mouselike Microchiroptera also receive some extra guidance from a remarkable physiological process known as echolocation. When flying in the dark, these bats emit high-frequency sounds and then use the echoes to determine distance and direction, as well as the size and movement of anything in front of them.

This "biological sonar system" is so refined that it can track the wing beats of a moth or something as fine as a human hair. Neuroethologists (people who study how nervous systems generate natural animal behavior) will tell you that our military doesn't even have sonar that sophisticated.

Bats have been the subject of myth, mystery, and misconception for centuries. Until recently, traditional thinking was that nocturnal bats could see at night but were blind by day. Now scientists at the Max Planck Institute for Brain Research in Frankfurt, Germany, and at The Field Museum of Natural History in Chicago have discovered that Megachiroptera bats have daylight vision, too. Apparently, this vision comes in handy for locating predators and even for socializing. Flying foxes don't sleep all day—they bounce from treetop to treetop for daytime confabs with their batty neighbors.

So there you have it: Bats can see, and they definitely know where they are going. The next time you want to use a creative—

though rather impolite—idiom to describe Aunt Millie's nearsightedness, you'd be more accurate to say she's "blind as a mole." That small, burrowing mammal has very small eyes and, indeed, very poor vision.

Q What's the weirdest creature in the sea?

A Once you hit a certain depth, every sea creature is weird. There's the terrifying angler fish, famous for its appearance in the movie *Finding Nemo*; the purple jellyfish, lighting up the sea like a Chinese lantern; the horrid stonefish, with a face only a mother could love; and the straight-out-of-science-fiction chimaera, or ghost shark, with its long snout and venomous dorsal spine.

Yes, there are a lot of "weirdest creature" candidates down there. For the winner, we're going with one of the ocean's lesser-known oddities: the ominous vampire squid.

The sole member of the order Vampyromorphida, the vampire squid's scientific name is *Vampyroteuthis infernalis,* which translates literally into "vampire squid from Hell." The squid is as black as night and has a pair of bloodshot eyes. Full-grown, the squid is no more than a foot long. For its size, it has the largest eyes of any animal in the world. Its ruby peepers are as large as a wolf's eyes, sometimes more than an inch in diameter.

Like many deep-sea denizens, the vampire squid has bioluminescent photophores all over its body. The squid can apparently turn these lights on and off at will, and it uses this ability—combined with the blackness of its skin against the utter dark of the deep— to attract and disorient its prey.

The vampire squid is not a true squid—the order Vampyromor- phida falls somewhere between the squid and the octopus—and so it does not possess an ink sac. In compensation, the vampire squid has the ability to expel a cloud of mucus when threatened; this mucus contains thousands of tiny bioluminescent orbs that serve to blind and confuse a predator while the vampire squid escapes into the shadows. As a second deterrent to predators, the vampire squid can turn itself inside out, exposing its suckers and cirri (tiny hair-like growths that act as tactile sensors) and making the creature look as though it is covered with spines.

Despite its name, the vampire squid does not feed on blood; its diet consists mostly of prawns and other tiny, floating creatures. Other than that, all that's missing for this Béla Lugosi mimic are the fangs and the widow's peak. But before you reach for a wooden stake, you should know that the vampire squid poses absolutely no threat to humans. It's found mostly at 1,500 to 2,500 feet below the surface, so the odds of encountering one are pretty slim.

Q Which snake toxin can kill you the fastest?

A A big, beautiful, olive-green serpent from the Australian outback is widely regarded as the deadliest (albeit not the most dangerous) snake on the planet. It's a good thing that the inland taipan is such a docile slitherer, because it is said that one of its bites contains enough venom to kill one hundred human adults.

No one knows for sure—when it comes to dangerous snakes, there's no shortage of wild claims (one British television program asserted that a dead rattlesnake could sense heat and would bite a warm object, like a hand)—but even the most sober herpetologists are in awe of the inland taipan. What scientists have verified is that the scaly denizen from Down Under, with its eyes of blackish brown and length that can reach twelve feet, pegs the venom meter.

In point of fact, that meter is a not-particularly-exact ratings method called LD50. It stands for "Lethal Dose, 50 percent" and measures how much venom is required to kill half the members of a test group within twenty-four hours. In this case, the members of the test group are mice, and inland taipan venom tops the LD50 list with only 0.025 milligram of venom needed per kilogram of mouse weight. The amount of venom in a single dose can kill 250,000 of the little critters. By comparison, the awful-sounding death adder's LD50 of 0.50 milligram per kilogram, which means it takes twenty times as much venom to kill half the test mice, makes this snake relatively benevolent, doing in a mere eleven to twelve thousand mice with the venom of one bite.

Some students of the reptile world say that a human adult who is bitten by an inland taipan would be dead in less than forty-five minutes. Actually, the human would have to be envenomated. Some killer snakes can sink their fangs into prey without injecting venom; it's what herpetologists call a "dry bite," or what lay-people call a "strong hint."

In any case, once envenomation occurs, the inland taipan's neurotoxin courses through the victim's lymph structure, attacking the nervous system until the muscles that control the lungs are paralyzed. (This is in contrast to the family of venomous snakes that inject a hemotoxin, which attacks the blood system.) Thankfully, not a single human fatality has been attributed to the inland taipan. It's a shy creature that feeds mostly on rats.

This isn't the case with the saw-scaled viper, which is found in India, Sri Lanka, parts of the Middle East, and in Africa north of the equator. A one-and-a-half-foot-long sienna-colored snake with long fangs, it makes a hissing sound when cornered by coiling into an S and rubbing its scales together. Its venom isn't as toxic as that of the inland taipan, but it is dangerous enough. This is the snake you don't want to meet in the grass. The saw-scaled viper, which is said to be responsible for more human deaths per year than any other snake, tops the list of dangerous serpents.

Chapter Three

LOVE AND LUST

Q Can a stripper write off
breast implants as a business expense?

A It's already been done. Several years ago, an exotic dancer
who went by the stage name Chesty Love persuaded a
tax appeals court to agree that her 56FF breasts were a capital
asset—a "stage prop," to be more specific—and to allow her
to write off the $2,088 it cost to get the twenty-pound set of
knockers installed. Word is, Chesty later tripped and ruptured
one of her props, but not before landing on every "goofiest tax
write-offs" list on earth.

It could be that the outlandishness of her props—and maybe
even a measure of feeling (amour? pity?) on the part of some

male judge—swayed the decision. You see, a Danish stripper who made the same claim in her country was turned down. "Most men like big breasts, and my employers also expect me to have a seductive chest," the disappointed Dane told reporters. "I had the operation for purely professional reasons."

True as the "professional reasons" assertion may be, the argument is vulnerable when you consider that plenty of strippers make good money without enlarged breasts—or so our friends tell us—and that codifying the rule would mean getting into a gray area of whether big breasts are more attractive than small ones. You might have to start defining what's "big." We assume the tax courts would rather leave that to frat boys.

Q Do blondes really have more fun?

A This question goes deeper than hair, and its answer is a bit off-color. Canadian anthropologist Peter Frost published a study in 2006 stating that at the end of the Ice Age, there was a shortage of men due to hunting deaths. This meant the remaining males had their pick of women—and the women they coveted had blonde hair. The vivid hair color, Frost suggested, sparked sexual arousal in the male brain.

Women, an intuitive bunch, picked up on this and ran with it. As the centuries passed, they tried different methods of lightening their hair, including high-alkaline soaps. But the resulting lighter hair color never looked quite right. Then, around the dawn of the twentieth century, women finally got what they desired: In 1909,

French chemist Eugene Schuller created a hair dye that delivered a more natural sheen. Schuller's success led him to form the L'Oreal Company.

From the onset of the twentieth century, Hollywood had a hand in promoting the idea that a woman who dyed her hair blonde was "fast." In the era of black-and-white movies, filmmakers discovered that blonde hair showed up better onscreen, and so the blonde bombshell was born. Movies that portrayed blondes as sexed-up and ready for action were popular for decades. This was particularly true in the 1950s with the rise of Marilyn Monroe, the queen of all sexed-up, fun-loving blondes.

The Clairol Company, which wanted to sell more hair dye, also contributed to placing the "blonde lifestyle" front and center. In 1955, the Foote, Cone & Belding ad agency was contracted by Clairol and put Shirley Polykoff on the job. She proceeded to conceive some of the most memorable slogans in the history of advertising.

The first of the series was, "Does she or doesn't she? Only her hairdresser knows for sure." Then Polykoff conceived, "If I've only one life...let me live it as a blonde." However, her most triumphant and oft-repeated slogan came in 1957: "Is it true blondes have more fun?"

When Polykoff took on the Clairol account, only 7 percent of American women dyed their hair. When she left the account in the 1970s, over 50 percent of American women did so. Polykoff's ads penetrated not only the follicles of millions of women, but they also ignited a debate that continues to this day: Do blondes have more fun?

According to the *Encyclopedia Britannica,* fun is "what provides amusement or enjoyment." Current blonde celebs such as Paris Hilton, Jessica Simpson, and Sienna Miller certainly seem to be living up to these words. So if you believe that fun is what provides amusement or enjoyment, then the blondes still have it.

Q Are oysters nature's Viagra?

A One of the most enduring food myths is that oysters have aphrodisiac properties. Many people swear that a plate of raw oysters can put even the coldest fish in the mood for love. Rumor has it that Casanova would dine on oysters before an amorous encounter. Some nut-jobs have even gone so far as to feed Viagra to oysters to increase the sexual power of the shellfish.

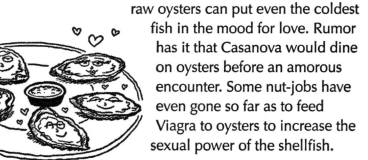

For years, scientists attempted to show that oysters don't have any libido-increasing abilities. A simple chemical analysis of an oyster reveals that it is made of nothing more than water, carbohydrates, protein, and trace amounts of sugars, fats, and minerals. None of these elements, whether taken separately or together, have been shown to have any effect on sexual desire or prowess.

But in 2005, at a meeting of the American Chemical Society, the oyster's sexual secrets were finally revealed. A group of American and Italian researchers discovered that the oyster belongs to a family of shellfish that has been shown to increase the release of certain sexual hormones. Oysters apparently contain amino acids that, when injected into rats, increase the levels of testosterone in males and progesterone in females. Elevated levels of these hormones in their respective genders have been linked to an increase in sexual activity.

So this myth appears to be grounded in fact. If you want to keep your libido humming, it might not be a bad idea to chow down on a dozen or so oysters.

Q Do most male prostitutes look like Richard Gere?

A Here's another example of Hollywood distorting public expectations. In the 1980 movie *American Gigolo,* Richard Gere plays a male prostitute who is so hot that women around him melt. Although less is known about male prostitution than female prostitution, look no further than another Gere vehicle, *Pretty Woman,* to see the dramatic disconnect between Tinseltown and reality. Do you think most female prostitutes look like Julia Roberts?

Don't dismiss the power of the media to reveal some truths about prostitutes, however. Direct your attention to the television show *COPS.* On any given night, you can tune in to a disturbing collection of professionals who are attempting to solicit money or drugs for sex. Most look like a cross between a liquefied wax figurine of Joan Rivers and a fetal pig. Not that we're putting down prostitutes.

Male prostitution is a time-honored profession. It dates back to ancient Greece, Rome, and just about anywhere there were men, women, and money. The modern gigolo business has grown a bit prickly, however. According to a recent government report from the Office of Juvenile Justice and Delinquency Prevention, male prostitutes are more likely than female prostitutes to get arrested, and police are less inclined to view them with sympathetic eyes.

As with female prostitutes, male hookers run the visual gamut. You have the movie star-type and the sixteen-year-old hayseed from Iowa who is fleeing his drunken father. What separates the two extremes? Money. A couple of sawbucks are not going to land you a night with a Dick Gere look-alike.

You have to be realistic when cruising the streets for hourly companionship. Prostitutes can't be expected to compete with the most beautiful stars of stage and screen. If they did, you probably couldn't afford them.

Q Do people lie on their online dating profiles?

A If you think the answer is no, you probably also believe that no one stretches the truth on a résumé or a tax return. Of course people lie on their online dating profiles!

Jeffrey Hancock, a professor of communication at Cornell University, has the proof. In a study on truthfulness in online dating that he completed in February 2007, Hancock found that it's fairly common for people to tell little white lies regarding their physical attributes.

Weight is a particularly touchy topic. Nearly two-thirds of the people in Hancock's study fudged their weight (64.1 percent of the women and 60.5 percent of the men). Height is another source of chicanery.

Thirty-nine percent of the women and 52.9 percent of the men surveyed were not entirely forthcoming about their stature. And then there's the matter of age, with 24.3 percent of the men and 13.1 percent of the women admitting to falsifying that number.

Fibs such as these are relatively harmless—unless, say, Tom, the potential object of your affection, turns out to be a 350-pound blimp rather than the svelte 175-pounder he said he was on his online dating profile. The deal-breakers often involve, er, weightier issues. Maybe you can get past Tom's blubber, but did he also lie about being gainfully employed and whether he's ever been convicted of a violent crime? If so, you'll obviously want to give Tom the boot.

The problem is that it's easy to lie on an online dating profile—it's as simple as a mouse click here and a mouse click there. People do it to bait the hook. Take Tom. He lied about his weight, his joblessness, and his rap sheet in order to pique your interest. Tom figured you'd overlook all of it once you got to know him and saw his heart of gold.

Who knows? Maybe you'll find the mate of your dreams on the Internet. Or maybe you'll find that lying sack Tom. When you're sifting through online dating profiles, you can never be sure.

Q Do women dress primarily for other women?

A Women must consider lots of factors when they peer into that closet every morning. They've got to dress for comfort and confidence—and a few compliments never hurt, especially if they come from other women.

Gals notice the good stuff. Little details like the lace and embroidery around your neckline, the haircalf trim on your handbag, how your jeans skim the floor at just the right length. Women know if you're wearing last season's Gucci or this year's Gap. And you can bet they'll judge you for it.

The guys? They don't care if your Prada is a replica or if hose and open-toe pumps are a faux pas. Are you showing a little leg or popping a plunging neckline? Bingo! You've earned admiration, acclaim, and a few free cosmos at the bar—especially if you're ovulating. That's right. According to a study conducted at UCLA and published in the journal *Hormones and Behavior* in 2006, women dress best when they're ready to mate.

The proof's in the pee stick. Researchers Martie Haselton and April Bleske-Rechek tracked thirty college coeds through an entire ovulatory cycle (they took urine tests to gauge where they were) and photographed each woman on high-fertility days and low-fertility days. The photos were shown to a panel of male and female judges who were asked, "In which photo is the person trying to look more attractive?"

Focusing on the clothes, jewelry, and hairstyles of the photographed women, the judges were more likely to deem the fertile-day photos more attractive. Researchers say that this suggests that when women are most fertile, their fashion sense is most keen.

"The closer women come to ovulation, the more attention they appear to pay to their appearance," says Haselton, the study's lead researcher and a UCLA associate professor of communication studies and psychology. "They tend to put on skirts instead of pants, show more skin, and generally dress more fashionably."

What is fashionable is certainly in the eye of the beholder. But this "reproductive" research builds upon previous studies showing that during their most fertile periods, women have an increased propensity to flirt with men. And we're talking men other than their boyfriends and husbands.

"Something in women's minds is tracking the ovulation cycle," Haselton says. "At some level, women 'know' when they are most fertile."

What they may or may not know is that besides dressing to impress other women, they're dressing to attract a male mate...at least a few days out of the month.

Q Do husbands and wives start looking alike?

A Have you ever met a married couple who looked so alike you could have sworn they were brother and sister? Well, scientific research has come up with a few explanations as to why.

For starters, it seems that we seek out mates who have features that are similar to our own. Recent studies suggest that we're attracted to those who look like us because they tend to have comparable personalities.

It's often said that women "marry their fathers." Research at the University of Pécs in Hungary supports this notion. Women tend to choose husbands who resemble their natural fathers—even if they're adopted. Scientists characterize it as "sexual imprinting," and it's known to occur in many animal species. Glenn Weisfeld, a human ethologist at Wayne State University in Detroit, says that there seems to be an advantage to selecting mates who are similar to ourselves: "Fortuitous genetic combinations" are retained in our offspring.

This doesn't give you carte blanche to marry your cute first cousin Betty. When it comes to mating, it's best to avoid people who are members of your family tree. But it doesn't hurt to pick a guy or gal who shares your dark features or toothy smile. Studies show that partners who are genetically similar to each other tend to have happier marriages.

It seems the longer couples stay together, the more their likenesses grow. A study by Robert Zajonc, a psychologist at the University of Michigan, found this to be the case—even among couples who didn't particularly look alike when they first got hitched. In Zajonc's study, people were presented with random photographs of men's and women's faces and asked to match up couples according to resemblance. Half of the photos were individual shots of couples that were taken when they were first married; the other half were individual shots of the same couples after twenty-five years of wedlock.

What do you know? People were able to match up husbands and wives far more often when looking at photo-graphs of the couples when they were older than when they were younger. It seems with time, the couples' similarities became much more discernible.

Why? Zajonc says husbands and wives start looking like each other because they spend decades sharing the same life experiences and emotions. Spouses often mimic the facial expressions of each other as a sign of empathy and closeness. Think of that the next time you and your spouse exchange smiles, sighs, or looks of contempt. Before you know it, you'll be sharing a life complete with matching facial sagging and wrinkle patterns! Hey, it's better than being told you look like your dog.

Q Why are we supposed to kiss under mistletoe?

A Kissing under mistletoe is meant to bring good luck and prosperity to those who are locking lips. It's a custom that might date back as far as AD 800, and originates from Norse folklore.

The legend holds that Balder the Good, the most beloved of the Norse gods, was killed at the hand of Hother (his blind brother). His weapon? A sprig of mistletoe. Balder was then brought back from the dead through the power of gifts that were showered upon his grave during the season of peace and goodwill. As a show of her gratitude, his mother, Frigg, hung mistletoe and kissed every person who walked under it, which reversed the plant's bad reputation.

Even earlier, around 200 BC, mistletoe was considered sacred in Norse culture. Druids, who were the polytheistic holy people for the Norse, thought mistletoe could cure diseases, improve fertility, and protect against black magic and evil forces. Druid priests, using golden sickles, ceremonially cut mistletoe branches from the oak trees (also considered holy) on which they grew and distributed them to be hung over doorways for protection. Mistletoe was believed to be so powerful that when enemies encountered each other under it, they were to put down their weapons and call a truce until the next day.

The Scandinavians, including the Danish, Swedish, and Norwegians—all descendants of the Norse—continued the belief that mistletoe was a plant of peace. People who were quarreling or couples who were at odds were to declare a truce when standing under mistletoe—and a kiss was the symbol of the truce. The Swedish were among the first Europeans to make their way to North America, in the early seventeenth century, and they brought this custom with them.

The traditional practice goes along these lines: Mistletoe is hung over a doorway. When two people of the opposite sex (remember, we're talking about the "traditional" practice) pass under it together, they are to kiss. The man then picks a berry from the sprig; when the branch is bare, no more kissing is to take place under that particular branch.

It is also said that if an unmarried woman passes under mistletoe without kissing, she will remain unwed for the whole of the following year; meanwhile, if a man and a women who are in love kiss under mistletoe, they will get married in the coming year. Another tradition involves burning mistletoe by the end of Christmas season (February 2). If the mistletoe isn't burned by then, all of the people who kissed beneath it will become enemies.

Q Why do men want to date fast women, but marry old-fashioned ones?

A The modern age has brought about modern marriages, so the adage about men wanting to marry old-fashioned girls can be thrown out the window. Of course, men still enjoy dating fast women. A woman quick to engage in a romp in the sack—or in the back of a taxi, if the opportunity should arise—will never have trouble finding a date.

The ideal of the father who strolls downstairs in the morning, pats the children atop their heads, slaps his wife on her derrière as she brandishes breakfast links, and whistles on his way to the family Ford in the driveway is only kept alive in the new millennium via sitcoms and TV commercials. We know this from U.S. Census Bureau statistics of 2002, which reported that only 7 percent of all households consisted of a married couple with children in which only the husband worked.

The ICM Research Company conducted a study in 2008 of nearly thirty million men and found that 69 percent of them longed for a woman who could manage the family's money; 59 percent wanted a woman who could stand up to him. These findings paint a clear picture that the majority of men don't want a submissive wife.

Neil Chethik has been studying male psychology since the early 1990s and conducted a survey while gathering data for the Men's Resource Center and a book called *VoiceMale: What Husbands Really Think About Their Marriages, Their Wives, Sex, Housework, and Commitment.* In his study, he discovered that 55 percent of married men were initially attracted to their wives because of their looks. However, Chethik found that less-tangible attributes—including a woman's attitude, bearing, and character—were ultimately what led the man down the aisle.

The National Marriage Project—an interdisciplinary initiative at Rutgers University—published *Sex Without Strings, Relationships Without Rings* in 2000. The study found that young people believe sex is for fun: "Both men and women regard casual sex as an expected part of the dating scene. Only a few take a moralistic stand against it." The study also indicated that the bar scene is a place for "casual sexual hookups, rather than finding a serious love interest." Chethik's research showed similar findings: Only 6 percent of the married men he surveyed said they met their spouses in a bar.

We can probably concur from the research that men like to date fast women. However, there is little evidence that men still want to marry old-fashioned women.

Chapter Four

ORIGINS AND TRADITIONS

Q Where did the F-word come from?

A There are hundreds of words that start with the letter F, but only one has the distinction of being *the* F-word. It's the mother of all epithets, the big one—the F-dash-dash-dash-word. We all know what it means, and we all know the various ways in which it can be used—but from where did it come?

According to the *Random House Historical Dictionary of American Slang,* published in 1994, the word is probably Germanic in origin. Its ancestors include the Middle Dutch word *fokken,* which means "to thrust, copulate with"; the Norwegian word *fukka,* meaning "to copulate"; and the Swedish words *focka* and *fock,* which translate to "to strike, push, copulate" and "penis," respectively.

Rooting out the etymology of dirty words is difficult because, well, they're dirty words. We live in a world today where the F-bomb is dropped repeatedly in books, in music, in movies, and on premium cable, but this has only been acceptable for the past thirty or forty years. In the early sixteenth century, which is thought to be the era into which the word was born, vulgarity was less acceptable in everyday speech. And in print? Forget about it. For this reason, historians have struggled to pinpoint how the F-word first came into use.

You may have heard that the F-word was born of an acronym, like scuba (self-contained underwater breathing apparatus). There are a couple of these legends floating around. The first has the word originally meaning "fornication under consent of the king." As the story goes, medieval couples needed royal permission to make a baby; while the couple was copulating inside, a placard was hung on their door that contained an acronym for the above phrase. According to the second theory, a placard with the same initials was hung around the necks of sexual criminals; in this case, they meant "for unlawful carnal knowledge."

While these are engaging stories—and popular, too—history presents a pretty strong case against them: Acronyms didn't become the basis for words until the early twentieth century, and people have been dropping the F-bomb for hundreds of years. It might seem extraordinary, but *the* F-word evolved just like every other F-word. It was adopted from another language and translated, and then it mutated into as many different uses as possible. And in this particular case, the uses are seemingly endless.

Q Do the kings and queens on playing cards represent anyone real?

A The beer is cold, the cigars are burning, and the wives are watching *Grey's Anatomy*. This can mean only one thing: poker night for the boys. And on this occasion, you're about to win a huge pile of chips because all the cards in your hand have faces on them. You lay the cards down, do a little bragging, and the fun goes on. But have you ever wondered whose faces are on those cards?

Some playing card enthusiasts swear that the kings and queens represent real figures from history. This isn't the case with today's playing cards—unless you get one of those decks that has the fifty-two greatest Notre Dame football players or fifty-two poses of Elvis Presley (skinny Elvis is always king). At one time, however, the pictures on playing cards did indeed depict real people.

Playing cards probably made their way to Europe from the Middle East during the fourteenth century. The Spaniards and the Italians were among the first Europeans to make playing cards, in the second half of the fourteenth century. But the French, who became the main producers of playing cards, jump-started the trend of using illustrations of real people.

In the fifteenth century, French card masters started creating pictorial identities for all the court cards. The card masters decided who would appear on the cards based, it appears, on nothing more than personal preference. Consider it the first political opinion poll. Apparently, some of the first kings to be represented on cards were Solomon, a king of Israel; Clovis, a king of the Franks; and Constantine, a Roman emperor.

During the lifetime of France's Henry IV (1553–1610), the cards were somewhat standardized. The kings most often represented were Charlemagne, a king of the Franks (hearts); David, a king of Israel (spades); Julius Caesar, a Roman emperor (diamonds); and Alexander, a king of Macedon (clubs).

The queens have been the objects of conjecture because the illustrations aren't as identifiable, although each had a name: The queen of hearts was Judith, who may have represented the Empress Judith of Bavaria; the queen of diamonds was Rachel, who may have represented the Biblical Rachel; the queen of spades was Pallas, who may have represented Joan of Arc or the Greek goddess Pallas Athena; and the queen of clubs was Argine, who may have represented the wife of Charles VII, king of France. There are other possibilities, too, ranging from Juno, the Roman queen of the Gods, to Agnes Sorel, the mistress of Charles VII.

Mistresses on playing cards? Think of the intrigue that would add to a poker night on Capitol Hill.

Q Aren't there better ways for Santa to sneak into a house than crawling down a chimney?

A Except for a few sour souls, everyone loves Santa Claus. How could you not? He spends his days in an enchanted world of elves and toys, he has a kick-ass flying sleigh, and he has the godlike ability to watch all the world's children at the same time. Yet for somebody who is supposed to be such a magical, all-knowing being, it appears that Santa Claus possibly isn't very bright. Case in point: this chimney business.

Come on, Claus. Do you really need to shimmy down a filthy chimney to deliver your presents? And with that ridiculous diet of cookies and milk, how much longer will you fit down it?

In Santa's defense, there's a lot of tradition behind his chimney act. Even though the image of the red velvet–clad Santa known to most Americans is a fairly recent development, the figure of Father Christmas is rooted in traditions dating back centuries. And 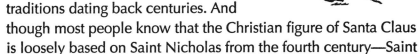 though most people know that the Christian figure of Santa Claus is loosely based on Saint Nicholas from the fourth century—Saint Nick is one of Santa's nicknames, after all—most of Santa's behavior, and magical powers are drawn from pagan sources.

Indeed, historians claim that not only Santa Claus, but also much of the holiday of Christmas itself is rooted in pagan tradition. Back in pre-Christian Europe, Germanic people celebrated the winter solstice at the end of December with a holiday known as Yule. Christmas, which later supplanted the pagan winter solstice festivals during the Christianization of Germanic people, maintained many of the pagan traditions. One was the belief that at Yule-time, the god Odin would ride a magical eight-legged horse through the sky. Children left food for the horse, which would be replaced by gifts from Odin, a custom that lives on today in the form of cookie bribery for Kris Kringle and his flying reindeer.

As for sliding down the chimney, folklorists point to another Germanic god: Hertha, the goddess of the home. In ancient pagan days, families gathered around the hearth during the winter solstice. A fire was made of evergreens, and the smoke beckoned Hertha, who entered the home through the chimney to grant winter solstice wishes.

It wasn't until 1822, when literature professor Clement Clarke Moore penned "Twas the Night Before Christmas," that Santa sliding down the chimney became a permanent fixture in popular Christmas tradition. Moore's poem became even more influential forty years later, when legendary cartoonist Thomas Nash illustrated it for *Harper's* magazine. In Nast's depiction, Santa was transformed from the skinny, somewhat creepy-looking figure of earlier traditions into a jolly, well-bearded soul. Despite Santa's physical transformation, other traits from his early incarnations linger, including the bewildering habit of crawling down chimneys.

But just because something is a habit doesn't make it excusable. The figure of Santa has morphed over the centuries, and there's no reason why he can't break the chimney routine in the future. Let's go, Santa—it's time to join the twenty-first century. And maybe check out the Zone Diet while you're at it.

Q How did crossword puzzles get started?

A They debuted as "word-cross" puzzles in December 1913. Arthur Wynne invented the first ones, which had no black squares. Three weeks after the first puzzle appeared in the *New York World,* a typesetter accidentally reversed the name, and "word-cross" became "cross word." Everyone liked the change.

Wynne edited the "Fun" section of the *New York World*. Born in Liverpool in 1862, he emigrated to the United States in 1905 and retired from the newspaper business five years after inventing the crossword puzzle. *The New York World* newspaper folded in 1931, and Wynne died in 1945. End of story? Not quite.

Wynne's contribution to American culture became a phenomenon. Dozens of newspapers constructed and ran their own weekly puzzles. By the early 1920s, crosswords were popular in Great Britain, Germany, France, and Russia.

In 1924, two New York entrepreneurs saw an opportunity. The story is that Richard Simon's aunt loved crossword puzzles and asked her nephew to find her a book of them. He couldn't, so he formed a company with partner Max Schuster and published the first crossword puzzle book. They printed 3,600 books on the first go-round, and America went crossword-crazy. Simon & Schuster reprinted and sold more than a quarter-million copies in the first year, and their upstart company is now one of the largest publishing houses in the world.

Q When the French swear, do they say, "Pardon my English"?

A They probably should, but they don't. The phrase "Pardon my French" has an elusive origin, but it likely grew out of the long-standing rivalry between England and France. As a result of their history of mutual contempt, each country's everyday language contains many stock phrases and terms that denigrate the other.

The French, for example, have long been thought of in the English mind as champions of indecency and lewdness. The terms "French pox" and "French disease" were used by the English to describe syphilis and other venereal diseases, beginning as early as the sixteenth century. And we only have to ponder the images evoked by phrases like "frenching," "French kiss," and "French tickler" to get a glimpse of France's reputation. (Okay, you can stop pondering the images now.)

But the French weren't about to take this lying down. One of their more inventive phrases was *les Anglais ont débarqué,* which translates to "the English have landed." Fair enough, until you learn that they used it to describe menstruation. This phrase probably stemmed from the bright red uniforms of the English soldiers who flooded into France to fight against Napoleon. The English were associated with an unwelcome crimson arrival, and this morphed into a euphemism for menstruation.

In the nineteenth century, both countries came up with similar terms for things, simply swapping "French" and "English" as appropriate. A "French letter," for example, was an English euphemism for a condom, while a Frenchman would have preferred a *capote anglaise* (an "English hood"). "To take French leave" means "to leave without saying goodbye"; *filer à l'anglais* means "to flee like the English."

There isn't a similar symmetry with the phrase "Pardon my French." When the French swear and decide to apologize—after all, many people swear constantly without feeling sorry about it—they generally say, *Excusez moi* ("excuse me"), or they use another faintly regretful phrase. Such a response is logical, but hardly insulting. And what fun is that?

Q If marbles are not made of marble, why are they called marbles?

A Because the name stuck, even if the use of actual marble to make the toys didn't.

The early Egyptians are thought to be the first to have played with small, round balls. Such scenes can be seen in their hieroglyphics, and rounded semi-precious stones were found in a child's tomb that dates to 3000 BC.

The ancient Romans also played marble-like games, which are mentioned frequently in the literature of the time. The round playing pieces were given as gifts during Saturnalia (the celebration of the winter solstice) mixed in a bag with nuts. Romans called the game they played "nuts," although the playing pieces were made from flint, stone, or baked clay.

As the Roman Empire spread across the land, so did this game. Over centuries, a variety of different stones—including marble— were used to make the playing pieces. In England, they were called "bowls" or "knickers." In about 1694, round balls made of marble were exported from Germany to England, complete with the name we know today: "marbles."

Using balls made of real marble, particularly white alabaster marble, made the game pricey. Substitutes that were more economical were used—including crockery, china, and clay—but some didn't work very well. Clay marbles, for example, sometimes broke apart during particularly spirited games. In the seventeen hundreds, glassmakers in Venice, Italy, began producing glass marbles, but it wasn't until the mid-eighteen hundreds that glass caught on. In about 1846 in Germany, special "marble scissors" were invented, making it cheaper to cut and manufacture the sturdy glass balls.

With the game now more affordable for the masses, glass marbles of all colors and designs spread throughout Europe and made their way to the United States. Clay marbles were being mass-produced in the United States by the late eighteen hundreds. They became known as "commies" because they were so common, and they remained popular until automated machines that shaped hot glass into marbles were introduced at the beginning of the twentieth century in Akron, Ohio. Akron was home to the vast majority of U.S. marble factories through at least the first half of the twentieth century, and the American Toy Marble Museum is located there today.

If you've never outgrown this simple game, you can call yourself a mibologist, or one who studies marbles. There are more of you out there than you'd think. Particularly in Akron.

Q What's inside a whole kit and caboodle?

A The real question is, what's not? The "whole kit and caboodle" is the works, the full treatment, the entirety, the whole lot, the whole schmear, the whole ball of wax, the whole nine yards, and the whole shebang!

And yes, the expression is pretty darn redundant. A kit is a collection of things; a caboodle is a collection of things. Sometimes a caboodle refers to a crowd or collection of people, too, but you get the point. The whole kit and caboodle is the greatest possible maximum whole of something, including everything and everyone connected with it.

As an expression, "the whole kit and caboodle" has evolved over time. Earlier variations are "the whole kit and boiling," "the whole kit and cargo," and "the whole kit and boodle." Boodle is thought to be derived from the early seventeenth-century Dutch *boedel* ("possessions") or the Old English *bottel* ("a bunch or a bundle").

"Kit and caboodle" is most likely a corrupted Americanism. This phrase was first recorded in the United States around the middle of the nineteenth century; it's believed that the "ka" sound was tacked on to "boodle" to make the most of euphony and alliteration. You must admit, "kit and caboodle" is a quite a catchy collection of locutions.

But back to the question: What's inside? Well, it could be a group or collection of infinite number. We're talking equipment, instruments, gizmos, gadgets, gangs, troupes, gear, tackle, hardware, paraphernalia, articles, items, artifacts, thingamabobs, thingamajigs, doohickeys, doodads, whatchamacallits, and all the tools of the trade. The whole kit and caboodle is sure to hold everything you'd ever need to do it yourself.

Back in the early nineteen hundreds, you could order a kit containing all the parts of an actual home from Sears, Roebuck &

Co. The "catalog kit homes," as they are now known, came with as many as thirty thousand numbered pieces, including beams, walls, flooring, nails, hinges, doorknobs, downspouts, plumbing pipes, shingles, and more. Weighing up to fifty thousand pounds, the house kit arrived at your nearest train depot.

Heck, Sears even threw in a pair of trees and a mortgage, if you needed one. Talk about the whole kit and caboodle. Or maybe you'd say the whole kit and colonial, the whole kit and cabin, the whole kit and cottage, the whole kit and Cape Cod...

Q Is it true that Eskimos have a thousand words for snow?

A It stands to reason that the Eskimos would have a lot of words for snow. Their lives revolve around the stuff, after all. But it seems that reports of the exact number of words have, well, snowballed.

There are five major Eskimo languages. The most widely used is Inuit, which is spoken by people living in northern Alaska, Canada, and Greenland. The notion that Eskimos have lots of words for snow started with anthropologist Frank Boas, who spent much of the late nineteenth century living with Eskimos in British Columbia and on Baffin Island of Upper Canada.

He wrote in the introduction to his 1911 *Handbook of North American Indians* that the Inuit language alone had four words for snow: *aput* ("snow on the ground"), *qana* ("falling snow"), *piqsirpoq* ("drifting snow"), and *qimuqsoq* ("a snowdrift").

Boas believed that differences in cultures were reflected in differences in language structure and usage. This wasn't to say that Inuits saw snow differently, according to Boas, but that they organized their thinking and their vocabulary about snow in a more complex manner because snow was such a big part of their daily lives.

In 1940, anthropologist Benjamin Whorf claimed that the Eskimo/Inuit language contained seven words for snow. In 1984, Steven Jacobson published the *Yup'ik Eskimo Dictionary,* which placed the figure for the Yup'ik Eskimos at well into the hundreds. Exaggeration piles upon exaggeration, and pretty soon a thousand words for snow sounds quite reasonable.

In a July 1991 article critiquing Jacobson's dictionary, University of Texas linguist Anthony Woodbury claimed the problem is lexemes. Lexemes are individual units of meaning: For example, the word "speak" can be transformed into the words spoken, speech, speaking, spoke, and so on. Woodbury noted that noun lexemes in at least one of the Eskimo languages can be arranged into more than 250 different individual words or phrases, and verbs allow for even more differentiations. He claimed that there were only fifteen individual lexemes for snow shared among the five Eskimo languages. That's not all that different from the English language.

Q Is there such a thing as a lucky number?

A Of course there is such a thing as a lucky number! How do you think those people who e-mail you every day with guaranteed winning lottery numbers get their information? It's not like they just make them up, right? Right?

Ever since people discovered counting, we have been obsessed with numbers. Scratches on cave walls and animals bones from tens of thousands of years ago marked the phases of the moon. In ancient Greek times, Pythagoras (he of the theorem that tormented you in high school geometry class) posited that all of the universe could be explained through numbers—he even founded a type of religion based on the principle. Later, Pythagorean-thought led to the development of numerology, a mystical practice that uses numbers to explore cosmology and relies heavily on the idea of "lucky" numbers.

Which numbers are lucky? That depends on where you live and the culture from which you come. As most people in Western civilization know, thirteen is a dreaded number (the number of diners at the Last Supper); in the Mayan civilization, on the other hand, thirteen was considered lucky (the number of months in the Mayan year and the number of Mayan gods). In Buddhist thought, four is a beneficial number (the Four Noble Truths); in China, however, four is associated with death.

As any craps player can tell you, seven is pretty lucky in Vegas; in northern China, though, it represents anger and abandon. Oh, and 666, the sign of the devil or antichrist in Christian lore? The Chinese think that it brings them good fortune. It's so lucky, in fact, that wealthy Chinese pay thousands of dollars for license plates with the number printed on it.

This is all well and good, but is there scientific evidence behind any of these lucky and unlucky numbers? We're not going to base our future lottery winnings on superstition, are we? The good news for empirically minded readers is that there are such things as lucky numbers in mathematics. The bad news is that they are based on a complicated aspect of number theory called a "sieve," which will leave average people befuddled. Regardless, there is no proof that these so-called lucky numbers actually bring you good luck.

Of course, who's to say? In 2005, a record 110 people claimed prizes of at least one hundred thousand dollars from the March 30 Powerball lottery drawing. How did they choose their numbers? From lucky numbers printed on the paper slips inside Chinese fortune cookies.

Q Shouldn't women receive a bachelorette's degree?

A Well, no. And it's only in the United States that someone would even ask that question.

The word "bachelor" derives from the Old French *bacheler,* meaning a young knight-in-training. Around 1300, it began to be used by English speakers for the same purpose. As the fourteenth century progressed, the word's definition expanded to include all types of young people who are learning a profession, including artisans and university students.

At this point in history, most people who fit this description were male, so it's easy to see how the word became associated with that gender. In fact, toward the end of the fourteenth century, the definition of bachelor once expanded again to refer to all unmarried men (not just those who were in the process of learning something).

In terms of academia, an undergraduate degree, which is usually earned after three, four, or five years of study (or should be, anyway—you know who you are, seventh-year seniors), was first known as a baccalaureate degree. This word has a similar root meaning to bachelor, as it comes from the Latin *baccalarius,* meaning "vassal farmer" or "farmer in training," and returns once again to the concept of beginning a journey of learning.

In modern English—drawing upon the Old English word for university students—a four-year undergraduate degree is known as a bachelor's degree (perhaps also indicating an optimistic hope that it will inspire a lifetime of knowledge-gathering). Because both men and women have been attending college since the eighteen hundreds, there is no gender distinction intended when this term is used in an academic setting.

The term "bachelorette," on the other hand, is laden with gender-related baggage. Its roots can be traced to the United States, circa 1935, when it entered modern parlance as an alternative to the more formal "bachelor-girl," which had developed to differentiate unmarried women from their male counterparts. The term was boosted to the forefront of our pop-culture dialect by Jim Lange, host of *The Dating Game,* a classic American game show that aired between 1965 and 1980.

The bottom line? Anyone who requests a bachelorette's degree come graduation day didn't learn much during all those years of college.

Q What is the rule of thumb?

A Here's what we know for sure: A "rule of thumb" is anything that is known by experience and not by science—it's something judged by approximation instead of exactitude. Here's what we don't know for sure: where this saying originated.

The most likely source of the idiom is the thumb's use as a general measuring tool, especially among carpenters. The length from the first joint of the thumb to its tip is approximately an inch. The thumb, then, is a built-in ruler. Other body parts have been used throughout history as measuring tools. A yard was once approximated as the length between the tip of a man's nose and the tips of his fingers when his arm was outstretched. Quite naturally, a foot arose from pacing off a distance. And the height of a horse is still measured in hands.

But back to thumbs. Purportedly, the rule of thumb once applied to wife-beaters, too. In England during the eighteenth century, a man was rumored to have been allowed under law to beat his wife with a stick, provided the stick was no thicker than his thumb. The thumb-to-stick rule was all the rage—or so the story goes. Whether such a law really existed remains uncertain, yet the legend took on a life of its own and persisted well into the twentieth century.

Indeed, in the 1970s legal activist Sheila Kuehl heard about the thumb-to-stick law and made it her personal mission to loudly and angrily condemn it everywhere she went. At any rate, there is no evidence that British women in the eighteenth century preferred marriage partners with skinny thumbs.

It is also unclear exactly when the rule of thumb came into being. As with seemingly everything in the Western world, it may have begun with the ancient Romans. By the time it found its way into print, it was used colloquially, the way we use it today. (The term first appeared in print in the late seventeenth century, in a book on fencing by Sir William Hope. According to his book, the master fencer does what he does by rule of thumb—meaning by practice and accumulated experience rather than by a particular model.)

So, what's the best way to correct someone who cites a false origin for this handy little idiom? Well, a rule of thumb is to avoid insulting his intelligence when suggesting that he might have the wrong idea.

Q How can it rain cats and dogs?

A It can't. Many of us are familiar with strange-but-true stories that describe fish, frogs, or bugs raining from the sky. Indeed, waterspouts and odd, windy weather patterns can suck up small animals, carry them a few miles, and drop them from the sky. But nowhere on record are confirmed reports of it raining felines and canines.

It's a figure of speech, and its origins unknown. However, that hasn't prevented etymologists from speculating. One unlikely theory claims that in days of yore, dogs and cats that were sleeping in the straw of thatched roofs would sometimes slip off the roof and fall to the ground during a rainstorm.

Almost as unlikely is the belief that the phrase was cobbled together from superstitions and mythology. Some cultures have associated cats with rain, and the Norse god Odin often was portrayed as being surrounded by dogs and wolves, which were associated with wind. (Anybody who's had an aging dog around the house can vouch for it being an occasional source of ill wind, but that's hardly the stuff of legend.) The components seem right with this one, but it's hard to imagine someone stitching everything together to coin a catchy phrase.

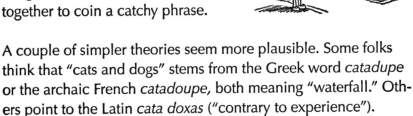

A couple of simpler theories seem more plausible. Some folks think that "cats and dogs" stems from the Greek word *catadupe* or the archaic French *catadoupe,* both meaning "waterfall." Others point to the Latin *cata doxas* ("contrary to experience").

The most believable explanation, however, is the least pleasant. The earliest uses of the term occur in English literature of the seventeenth and eighteenth centuries. Around that time in London, dead animals, including cats and dogs, were thrown out with the trash. Rains would sweep up the carcasses and wash them through the streets. Jonathan Swift used the phrase "rain cats and dogs" in his book *A Complete Collection of Polite and Ingenious Conversation* in 1738. Twenty-eight years earlier, Swift had published a poem, "A Description of a City Shower," that included the lines: "Drown'd Puppies, stinking Sprats, all drench'd in Mud/ Dead Cats and Turnip-Tops come tumbling down the Flood."

Hardly a love sonnet, but perhaps it answers our question.

Q What is the difference between a city mile and a country mile?

A In some countries, the mile is a standard unit of measure for a distance that equals 5,280 feet. Why it's 5,280 feet can be traced to the ancient Britons. Freed from Roman rule, the Britons decided upon a compromise between the Roman *mille passus* (a thousand paces, which was five thousand Roman feet) and their furlong (660 British feet, which naturally differed slightly in length from a Roman foot). The statute mile (now called the international mile) is 5,280 feet, or eight furlongs.

If that weren't confusing enough, there are different kinds of miles: the nautical mile, the geographical mile, the air mile, the metric mile. One you won't usually see, however, is the country mile. That's because it has no numeric definition. The *Merriam-Webster Online Dictionary* dates the term to about 1950, and most dictionaries say that "country mile" is informal and used to denote "a long distance."

Does this mean that miles are longer in the country than else-where? Although the origin of the phrase is unknown, there are several theories about its meaning. One holds that in times during which people walked nearly everywhere, a mile didn't seem very far. In the era of cars and mass transportation associated with city living, walking a mile is a bigger deal.

Another possibility relates to the grid systems of streets in many cities versus the meandering roads often found in the country. The shortest distance between two points is a straight line, but rural roads sometimes are anything but straight. So it can in fact take you longer to get from one place to another in the country, where two points that are a mile apart may not be connected by a straight road.

So if you have to go a country mile, you should be prepared for a long journey.

Q What's so lucky about a four-leaf clover?

A Before we address this question, another should really be answered: What is luck?

Luck, quite simply, is beating the odds. For instance, it's the rareness of a winning lottery ticket that makes it so extraordinary and, well, lucky. The same goes for four-leaf clovers. A four-leaf clover is a genetic mutation of the three-leaf *trifolium repens* (white clover) that occurs once every ten thousand times in nature. One four-leaf clover; 9,999 three-leaf clovers. Not quite the same odds as the lottery, but rare nonetheless.

The early Celts of Great Britain thought that anyone who found a four-leaf clover was lucky. More specifically, they believed that the special quality of the clover allowed them to see evil spirits and, therefore, be protected from them.

When Saint Patrick came to Ireland from Scotland in the fifth century to convert the Irish to Christianity, legend says that he used the three-leaf clover to explain the trinity of the Father, Son, and Holy Ghost to the pagan Celts. The three-leaf shamrock soon became the symbol of a Christian Ireland.

What about the fourth leaf—what does it represent? The fourth leaf has been associated with God's grace, happiness, or, not surprisingly, luck. Legend has it that the four-leaf clover protects against snakes, and that Saint Patrick himself expelled all of the snakes from Ireland. Ah, those lucky Irish. Did Saint Patrick use a four-leaf clover? We're not sure, but we know this much: Ireland has no indigenous snakes.

Today, the four-leaf clover is considered as lucky as ever, but be wary of counterfeits. If you walk into almost any flower shop in early spring, you'll find pots of what look to be four-leaf clovers being sold as "lucky" plants. These aren't real clovers but *oxalis deppei* or *marsilea quadrifolia,* which always have four leaves. That's hardly beating the odds.

Q What's that Christmas tree doing on top of that unfinished building?

A Circa 621 BC, upon completion of a bridge crossing the Tiber River, the Romans tossed people into the water as a sacrifice to the gods. In the Middle Ages, a priest would be present at the ceremony that celebrated the end of a construction project in order to bless the finished product. In modern times, the practice has changed, but the purpose remains the same: We have the topping-off ceremony.

When it comes time to raise the final steel beam, which is also the highest beam in the skeletal structure of a new building, construction workers sign the beam and adorn it with an evergreen and an American flag. The custom dates back to the 1920s in the

United States; in the rest of the world—specifically, in Europe—it goes back much further. (The color and design of the flag, obviously, varies from country to country.)

The topping-off ceremony means different things to different people. It can be a sacred rite intended to keep evil spirits away from the new building. On a simpler level, it might signify the successful end of one stage of the construction process while simultaneously announcing the commencement of a new stage. It is a sign that the venture has thus far been a safe one, with no fatalities; or it commemorates workers who died along the way. One theme remains constant: The evergreen tree and the flag represent the hope that the rest of the project will be blessed with good fortune.

Speaking of good fortune, modern-day construction workers undoubtedly feel blessed that human sacrifices are no longer part of the tradition. Who, after all, wants to be heaved from a tall building?

Q How can a penny be bad?

A Pennies may be lucky, but they certainly aren't bad. In the aphorism "A bad penny always turns up," the penny is standing in for a person. It's a way of saying a scoundrel will keep coming back no matter how many times he's sent away.

The saying originated in England, where men were sometimes referred to as shillings, an allusion to the amount per day an enlisted man was paid to serve the crown. A "bad shilling" was a man who was lazy, incompetent, or immoral. When this aphorism made the trans-Atlantic jump from England to America, so did the language of the currency, and "bad shilling" became "bad penny."

The saying is also related to the phrase "taking the king's shilling," which dates to 1707. To take the king's shilling was to enlist in the military, where a soldier was compensated a shilling per day. Comparing men to money dates back to the ancient Romans: "Soldier" comes from *solidus,* which was the gold coin that enlisted men were given as compensation.

American soldiers have never been paid in pennies, and American people have never been referred to as pennies, but the phrase—like the penny to which it refers—turns up from time to time.

Chapter Five

PEOPLE

Q **Wouldn't the Gerber baby be a grandparent by now?**

A It's the face that launched a thousand spoons. That cute cherubic mug first appeared on Gerber baby food products and advertisements in 1928 as the winner of a contest to find the perfect face to promote strained peas. Response to the picture was so positive that by 1931, Gerber had adopted the image as its official trademark. It has appeared on all Gerber products ever since.

Over the years, rumors spread as people tried to guess the identity of the model. Humphrey Bogart, Shirley Temple, Elizabeth Taylor, and Bob Dole (Bob Dole?!) were popular suggestions.

Sure, those people may have had somewhat attractive faces as babies—but everyone knows that writers are the most beautiful people in the world, and so it makes sense that the mysterious Gerber baby grew up to be mystery novelist Ann Turner Cook of Tampa, Florida. A retired high school English teacher, Cook authored the Brandy O'Bannon series of murder-mystery novels.

Cook was four months old back in 1927 when a neighbor, artist Dorothy Hope Smith, used her as the model for an entry in the Gerber baby-picture contest. Smith submitted a charcoal sketch that she planned to flesh out as a painting later, but the folks at Gerber liked the original just fine. Cook's identity wasn't a big secret. Her four children delighted in telling their friends about their mother's claim to fame, and her students sometimes teased her about it. Her renown grew quite a bit in December 1996, when she was on hand to help Gerber launch an updated version of its packaging that nonetheless retained the famous original image.

And to answer the question: Yes. At last count, the Gerber baby had ten grandchildren.

Q Are left-handed people evil?

A Poor lefties. Their dominant hand has suffered centuries of bad press, beginning in Biblical times. Take the parable of

the sheep and the goats (Matthew 25:31–46). The she
on Christ's right hand and the goats on the left. In the ___, those
on the right inherit the kingdom of God, and those on the left
inherit third-degree burns. That's right—they're sent packing to
the everlasting fire.

You have to admit, Christianity does seem a bit slanted toward the
right. The right hand gives the blessing and makes the sign of the
cross. And "the right hand of the Lord doeth valiantly. The right
hand of the Lord is exalted" (Psalm 118:15–16). As a matter of
fact, the Bible contains twenty-five unfavorable references to the
left hand, compared to more than one hundred favorable references to the right.

Yes, people have actually counted the Biblical mentions—and
you can bet they weren't southpaws, who have suffered plenty of
other indignities, such as being forced to cut with right-handed
scissors and sit at a right-handed desk. So if right-handedness is
next to Godliness, where does that leave the left? Well, the left is
a symbol of Satan himself. The Prince of Darkness is almost always portrayed as a lefthander. As for evil spirits, they like to lurk
on the left side, too. That's why you throw spilled salt over your
left shoulder to ward them off.

It doesn't help that common language literally defines left-hand-
edness as dishonorable. The Latin word for left, sinistra, is actually where we get the English adjective "sinister." Look up "left-
handed" in the dictionary and you'll encounter plenty of cynical
synonyms, like "backhanded," "dubious," and "insincere." Other
languages translate no better. The Greek term for left-handed,
skaios, means "ill-omened" or "awkward." The French gauche
translates to "awkward" or "clumsy."

From a numbers point of view, about 10 percent of the world's population is left-handed. So is there any science to support the idea that they're all a bunch of depraved fiends? Of course not. But statistically, lefties are more likely to suffer all kinds of disorders, from bed-wetting and dyslexia to alcoholism and schizophrenia. As if that weren't bad enough, lefties have a better chance than righties of dying young and of getting into accidents.

However, to balance the scales in the southpaws' favor, psychological studies have found that lefties are more common among groups of highly talented and creative people. Tests have shown there are more lefties than righties with IQs higher than 140 (that's a score of "genius" or "near genius").

The most famous minds of the left-handed persuasion are Albert Einstein, Isaac Newton, Benjamin Franklin, Leonardo da Vinci, and Michelangelo. To give credit where credit is due, lefties have contributed a lot of good to this world. Toss them a compliment every once in a while. Just make sure it's not a left-handed one.

Q Who was the real McCoy?

A This question doesn't have a definitive answer, although that hasn't stopped people from trying to find one. The phrase itself is invoked whenever a question of authenticity is raised. Given several options, the one true selection is referred to as "the real McCoy," meaning it is the genuine article and you should accept no substitute. But who is this McCoy fellow, and what makes him so real?

One of the most believable accounts involves a boxer who was active around the turn of the twentieth century. Norman Selby, who boxed under the name "Kid McCoy," was a frequent source of imitation, and it's said that he adopted the phrase "the Real McCoy" to distinguish himself from the drove of impostors.

Another explanation states that a brand of Scottish whiskey used the phrase as part of an advertising campaign, starting in 1870. G. Mackay & Co. Ltd. referred to itself as "the real Mackay," which is, of course, an alternate spelling (and pronunciation) of the now-popular idiom.

And then there's a theory that originates in the United States' prohibition period of the 1920s and 1930s. During this time, bootleg alcohol was quite a profitable business for those who weren't afraid to take some risks. It was even more profitable for the bootleggers who watered down their booze.

One man, however, wouldn't compromise the quality of the liquor he sold—you guessed it, a fellow named McCoy. Bill McCoy. He earned a hardy reputation by sailing between Canada and the United States with contraband rum or whiskey on board. Shrewdly, McCoy dropped anchor in international waters (usually just outside Boston, New York City, or Philadelphia), where prohibition laws weren't in effect, and sold his wares legally to those who sailed out to him.

Although he might have made more money in the short term by watering down the booze he sold, McCoy was in it for the long haul and refused to taint his product. Therefore, the goods from his ship came to be known as "the real McCoy"—there was no diluted booze in McCoy's bottles.

So, who was the *real* McCoy? We may never know for sure. It appears there were several.

Q Did Lady Godiva really ride in the nude?

A Imagine a beautiful, long-haired woman riding a horse through the center of town—in the nude. It's quite an image. But is the ride of Lady Godiva just a legend? Was there really such a person, and did she give new meaning to the notion of riding bareback?

Indeed, there was a Lady Godiva. She was the wife of Leofric, Earl of Mercia, and she lived in the eleventh century near the town of Coventry, England. She supposedly was extremely pious, a patron of the church, and instrumental in the building of several abbeys. Some writings portray Leofric as equally religious, though not very generous toward "the little people." At one point, he levied a huge tax on the citizens of Coventry. Godiva felt awful for the townspeople and begged her husband to repeal the tax. Leofric said he would remove the tax if Godiva stripped naked and rode her horse through the streets of Coventry. Godiva declared the streets be cleared, let down her long hair to cover her body, and did the deed while accompanied by two knights. Leofric kept his word and rolled back the tax.

In another version of the story, Godiva was a patron of the arts. Leofric, who was not, convinced his wife to go on her ride by pointing out the Greek and Roman celebrations of the nude form as a work of art.

There's really no way to know for certain if Godiva's ride happened. The chronicler at the abbey in nearby Evesham didn't mention it in his eleventh-century writings about Leofric and Godiva. No contemporaries wrote of it either. It wasn't written about until much later—in the thirteenth century—by Roger of Wendover. However, Roger's writings are known to be full of exaggerations and biases rather than historical facts.

Later writers, such as Matthew of Westminster in the fourteenth century, implied that a miracle kept the townspeople from seeing Godiva in the nude. Some later writers said Leofric was a persecutor of the church but underwent a religious conversion because of this miracle. So although there is no proof of the ride, the legend lives.

Colleges and chocolate companies employ Godiva logos. And in Coventry, her ride is commemorated each year as part of a festival. Not usually in the nude, though.

Q Did P. T. Barnum really say, "There's a sucker born every minute"?

A Good old Phineas Taylor Barnum, the great-great-grandfather of the great all-American scam. The head huckster who told us, "There's a sucker born every minute."

Or did he?

Many contemporary historians believe that Barnum has been unfairly maligned. Rick Brown, founder of the Newspaper Collectors Society of America and Historybuff.com, fingers David Hannum as the real culprit. In 1869, Hannum was part of a group that was making a mint exhibiting a huge stone figure it claimed was a bona fide petrified giant, unearthed by a farmer in Cardiff, New York. Always on the lookout for new exhibits to add to his American Museum, Barnum offered fifty thousand dollars for the unusual specimen. (That's more than two million dollars today.)

When Hannum & Co. turned him down, Barnum "dug up" his own giant and announced that Hannum's was a fake. Hannum quickly retaliated with a lawsuit. Before the case could be re-solved, amateur archaeologist George Hull came forward with the astounding confession that he himself had paid to have the Cardiff giant carved from gypsum, buried, and subsequently discovered. In other words, the whole thing was a hoax. Somewhere in this comedy of errors, Hannum is reputed to have said, "There's a sucker born every minute."

It's also possible that the famous saying came from Joseph Bes-simer, otherwise known as "Paper Collar Joe," a notorious con man of the late nineteenth century. Joe may have had a paper collar, but unfortunately, he left no paper trail to document his statement, so we're stuck with historical rumor.

Why is the quote attributed to Barnum? Adam Forepaugh, a rival circus owner, may have attributed the words to Barnum in the 1880s in an attempt to smear his competitor's reputation.

Legendarily, Barnum wasn't above pulling a few fast ones. He posted a sign at his sideshow that read, "This Way to the Egress," banking on the assumption that most visitors wouldn't know "egress" is a synonym for "exit" and wouldn't find out until they were back out on the street and had to pay for another ticket if they wanted to continue their tour.

But Barnum knew where to draw the line. He was a believer in what he called "humbug," or the art of putting on "glittering appearances." Humbug was not out-and-out dishonesty—it was entertainment. "I don't believe in duping the public, but I do believe in first attracting them and then pleasing them," he wrote to a publisher in 1860. People wouldn't mind being deceived, he surmised, as long they felt they had gotten their money's worth.

How right was he? It's easy to test his hypothesis. Your laboratory is right in your living room. It's called TV.

Q How come you never see famous people on jury duty?

A When people are summoned for jury duty, they are actually being summoned for a jury-selection process. If the case requires twelve people on the jury (most states use twelve jurors for trials, but some use six, especially in civil cases), the court may call in eighty people as potential jurors. The group then gets pared to eighteen (including six alternates).

If you think of jury duty as having to go to the courthouse for a day to take part in that selection process, celebrities do have to participate. Robert De Niro, Brad Pitt, Mariah Carey, Jerry Seinfeld, Uma Thurman, and scores of other celebs have been called to jury duty. Whether they end up serving on a jury is a different matter altogether.

For starters, anyone can stall a jury duty summons for quite some time before running out of excuses. A simple phone call can get you a six-month respite, no questions asked. After that, there has to be a pretty good reason why you can't perform this civic duty.

At the jury selection, celebrities often argue their ways out of serving. Woody Allen sent a letter saying that he'd had a traumatic experience in court during a child-custody case with Mia Farrow and couldn't bear being in a courtroom again. The authorities didn't buy it, and he was ordered to show up. He arrived with his lawyer, his agent, and his bodyguard and refused to sit with other potential jurors, opting instead to stand. Eventually, he was allowed to leave. If acting like an arrogant celebrity doesn't work, there's always the chance that either side's attorney will dismiss the celebrity if the attorney thinks that the celebrity will influence the trial.

Sometimes celebrities are selected for a jury, though. In 2004 Oprah Winfrey served for a murder trial, and Rudolph Giuliani served for a minor trial in 1999 while he was mayor of New York. The trial involved a man who claimed that scalding hot shower water from an improperly maintained water heater burned his genitals, causing him to become impotent. The jury ruled against him.

Q Was Wyatt Earp married to a hooker?

A Wyatt Earp was apparently quick on the draw when it came to marriage, too; the Wild West icon had three wives over the course of his life. And of the three Mrs. Earps, only one was *not* suspected of being or of having been a prostitute.

Wyatt's first wife, Urilla, died within a year of their marriage. No one has ever said a word against her. In fact, the information about Urilla is so sparse that most people don't have a word to say about her, period.

Wyatt's second wife, Celia Ann "Mattie" Blaylock, was a teenage runaway who had settled in Dodge City, Kansas. No proof exists—brothels are not known for their scrupulous record-keeping, after all—but the circumstances suggest that Mattie was a "woman of easy virtue." She and Wyatt presented themselves as a married couple in Kansas, New Mexico, and Arizona, although no marriage license or divorce decree ever surfaced.

In Tombstone, Arizona, Wyatt met the woman with whom he would spend the rest of his life: Josephine "Sadie" Marcus. Sadie claimed to be an actress who'd settled in Tombstone, and she kept company with the local sheriff, John Behan, but rumors about her real profession have never been quieted. Was she a prostitute, Behan's mistress, or a traveling actress who was enjoying a fling in Tombstone? No one is sure.

When Wyatt wooed Sadie away from Sheriff Behan, Mattie was furious. She had left town after the infamous shootout at the OK Corral and the murder of Wyatt's brother Morgan, but she expected to return to her husband when the threats against his family settled down. In the interim, though, Wyatt openly took up with Sadie and would have nothing more to do with the purported former Mrs. Earp. A pathetic Mattie, who was addicted to alcohol and laudanum (a liquid form of opium), drifted among the two-bit mining towns of Arizona and probably supported herself by plying the world's oldest profession. She died of a drug overdose—which was officially ruled a suicide—six years after Wyatt abandoned her.

Sadie and Wyatt Earp remained together until Wyatt's death in 1929—nearly fifty years. No marriage license exists for them. Sadie claimed that they were hitched aboard a yacht outside the three-mile limit of U.S. territory.

Chapter Six

FOOD AND DRINK

Q Is chicken soup really good for a cold?

A Well, an Egyptian rabbi, physician, and philosopher named Moshe ben Maimonides seemed to think so. He was the first to prescribe chicken soup as a cold and asthma remedy—and that was way back in the twelfth century.

Since then, mothers and grandmothers worldwide have been pushing bowls of homemade broth to cure everything from colds, flus, and stomach problems to severely broken hearts. It's no surprise, then, that chicken soup is often referred to by another name: Jewish penicillin.

Until recently, there was little scientific literature to explain how or why chicken soup seems to make us feel better. Some suspected that hot steam from the soup worked to open congested airways. Others believed that it was simply a matter of receiving some much-needed attention and TLC.

There's probably some truth to both of these theories, but in 2000 a team at the University of Nebraska Medical Center provided a more substantial answer. It all began when Dr. Stephen Rennard, a researcher and specialist in pulmonary medicine, brought a batch of his wife's homemade chicken soup into the lab. It was her Lithuanian grandmother's recipe—a medley of chicken, onions, sweet potatoes, parsnips, turnips, carrots, celery stems, parsley, and matzo balls.

After running numerous laboratory tests on it, Rennard and his colleagues determined that chicken soup contains several ingredients with "beneficial medicinal activity." Specifically, the soup blocks the movement of inflammatory cells called neutrophils.

Why is this important? Neutrophils are responsible for stimulating the production of mucus. By limiting the movement of neutrophils, chicken soup helps reduce the horrid inflammation and congestion associated with colds and upper respiratory infections. While it is not a cure, a bowl of chicken soup can make your nose less stuffy, your throat less sore, and your cough less hacking.

And the good news is that chicken soup doesn't have to be homemade to help you out. As a point of comparison, Rennard tested thirteen different commercial brands of chicken soup commonly found at the grocery store. He discovered that all except one (chicken-flavored ramen noodles) relieved the inflammation associated with colds. But did any of them taste as good as Grandma's?

Q What exactly is a calorie?

A A large orange has about 85; a large order of French fries can have as many as 575. It's hard enough to count calories, let alone understand them. But maybe the effort will help you burn an extra few.

By definition, a calorie is the amount of heat needed to raise the temperature of a liter of water by one degree Celsius. If that sends your mind spinning back to the unspeakable horrors of high school chem lab, think of it this way: A calorie is not a tangible thing, but a unit of measurement. More specifically, it's a scientific means of measuring energy.

When we hear the word calorie, we almost always associate it with food. However, calories apply to everything containing energy. For example, there are about thirty-one million calories in a gallon of gasoline. But here's where it gets a bit tricky. The calories in that gallon of gasoline are officially spelled with a lowercase c. These small-c calories are units of measurement used only by chemists.

However, nutritionists and scientists who measure the energy found in food officially use a capital C to indicate kilocalories (abbreviated kcal or Kcal). There are a thousand small-c calories in one big-C Calorie, or kilocalorie. On nutrition labels in the United States, calorie and Calorie are often used interchangeably, but now you know, at least in scientific terms, that's flat-out wrong. One is a unit of measure that is a thousand times greater than the other.

Anyway, when you check the nutritional information on the back of your Hershey's bar wrapper and it says 270 calories, you're being told how much energy your body could potentially get from eating the candy. Once consumed, this energy is either burned through your body's physical processes and activity or converted into fat for later use.

The simple truth is, everything we do relies on the energy that comes from calories; our bodies require calories just to keep our hearts pumping. Most people can take in about two to three thousand calories per day—that's enough energy to boil twenty to thirty quarts of water—and still maintain their current body weight.

It's when we go above our caloric needs that our bellies begin to bulge. If you take in an extra 3,500 calories (about fourteen slices of hand-tossed pepperoni pizza), you'll gain a pound—and develop a case of indigestion.

Q What is the oldest still-popular alcoholic beverage?

A That would be beer, the alcoholic beverage of choice for millions of thirsty folks dotting the globe.

Beer dates back at least to the sixth millennium BC in Mesopotamia, a region located for the most part in what is today Iraq, which brings up a logical question: Why do humans still drink zestless Bud Light in mass quantities despite the fact that they have had more than seven millennia to refine their taste in beer? Perhaps the Sumerian goddess Ninkasi would know: The Sumerian hymn to her is also a recipe for beer itself.

It's been speculated that beer was discovered by accident, when some bread dough was left out in a Sumerian courtyard, was rained on, and fermented into a beerlike liquid over the next several days. If that's true, it's a charming bit of good luck for mankind. But even more thought-provoking is this golden nugget of information: It is widely believed that bread and beer were the catalysts for civilization.

Until humans discovered that certain grains could be made into bread and beer, they were nomadic wanderers. Once they lucked into the earliest ancestors of Wonder Bread and Pabst Blue Ribbon, they settled down into communities that shared efforts in cultivating and selling grain, and produced food on the spot. In this epochal light, the annual Super Bowl "Bud Bowl" ads seem a bit shallow, no?

Anyhow, despite its exalted position in human history and football, beer isn't the oldest known booze. That would be a Chinese rice wine sweetened in the making with fruit and honey. It was discovered in 2004, its molecules clinging to nine-thousand-year-old pot fragments from a Stone Age site in northern China. In other words, it's probably about a thousand years older than beer.

Take that, Augie Busch

Q Is Jell-O made from horses?

A Could this fun, wiggly dessert be the final resting place for the likes of Black Beauty and Mister Ed? Sure. But let's not be too picky—any creature with bones can become Jell-O. It's an equal opportunity dessert.

Jell-O is made from gelatin, which is processed collagen. Collagen makes your bones strong and your skin elastic and stretchy (there's that jiggly wiggle). To make gelatin, you take bones, skin, tendons, and whatnot from animals (primarily cows or pigs), grind everything up, wash and soak it in acid (and also lime, if cow parts are used), and throw it in a vat to boil. The acid or lime breaks down the components of the ground animal pieces, and the result is gelatin, among other things. The gelatin conveniently rises to the top of this mixture of acid and animal parts, creating an easy-to-remove film.

In the Victorian era, when gelatin was really catching on, it was sold in the film state. People had to clarify the gelatin by boiling it with egg whites and eggshells, which took a lot of time. In 1845, a crafty inventor patented a powdered gelatin, which was to be extracted from the bones of geese. In 1897, this powdered gelatin was named Jell-O and went on to become the line of dessert products that, to this day, we always have room for.

Why does the list of ingredients in Jell-O include gelatin and not cow and pig pieces? Because the U.S. federal government does not consider gelatin an animal product, since it is extensively processed. Gelatin is also found in gummy bears candy, cream cheese, marshmallows, and other foods.

What if you like Jell-O, cream cheese, marshmallows, and such, but would rather not eat the boiled bones and skin of animals? There are alternatives. Agar and carrageenan are made from seaweed and can be used to create delicious gelatin-like goodies.

So while it's unlikely your Jell-O contains traces of Mister Ed or Black Beauty, it could test positive for Wilbur or Elsie.

Q Can you be allergic to water?

A Technically, you can be allergic to water. But it's so rare that there is only one person on record—Heidi Falconer of Shropshire, England—to have been born with the condition, which is called *aquagenous urticaria* or *aquagenic urticaria*. Only thirty people around the world have been diagnosed with water allergy (whether congenital or developed later in life).

For these few, when water—even sweat and tears—touches the skin or mucous membranes, the skin becomes itchy and the sufferer breaks out in a rash and/or blisters. These symptoms typically appear within a few minutes and clear up within two hours. But severe responses can cause a life-threatening condition, anaphylaxis, in which the airways swell and close.

Depending on the severity of the condition, the sufferer may still be able to take showers without applying a protective barrier.

Ashleigh Morris of Melbourne, Australia, for example, has roughly one minute to take a shower before risking a severe reaction. As for Heidi Falconer, she has to use a special cream, applied every four hours, that is made in Sweden and prevents water from touching her skin. It's the only way Heidi can take a shower or do other things that involve contact with water.

You may be wondering if people who are allergic to water can drink water. They can't. But they can drink small amounts of milk and pure orange juice.

There is no known cure for *aquagenous urticaria*. However, doctors have managed to evaluate possible causes on a case-by-case basis. In Heidi Falconer's case, doctors think that unusual proteins in her system react to water. In Ashleigh Morris's case, her dermatologist concluded that a reaction to penicillin caused her to develop the water allergy.

Either way, a life without water is a tough life indeed.

Q What's so hot about a hot dog?

A Honestly? Not much. The "hot" in hot dog doesn't mean spicy, sexy, stolen, or anything that super exciting. It's just a reference to the way the sausages are served. And that would be warm, and preferably in a soft, sliced bun.

What really gets people hot—as in, riled up—is how the term "hot dog" came about. It's agreed that the hot dog, a.k.a. frankfurter, originated in Germany. Some say it was first made in Frankfurt am Main around 1484; others insist it was in Coburg in the late sixteen hundreds. At any rate, what really matters is that the Germans referred to their skinny sausage creation as "dachshund" or "little dog" sausage. This was most certainly a nod to their country's popular short-legged, long-bodied dog breed.

Dachshunds also go by the nickname of "wiener dogs," and whaddaya know—hot dogs are known as wieners, too. And no, this doesn't mean that hot dogs are made from dog meat. American hot dogs can be crafted from beef, pork, veal, chicken, turkey, or any or all of the above. Now we know that "dog" was a longtime common synonym for sausage, but just when did the "hot" come into play? Many sources credit American journalist and cartoonist Thomas Aloysius Dorgan, or TAD, for coining the term. (This guy is also credited with coming up with such phrases as "the cat's meow" and "for crying out loud.")

On a chilly day at New York's Polo Grounds in April 1901, according to the National Hot Dog & Sausage Council, vendors weren't making any money on the usual frozen ice cream and cold soda, so they started selling dachshund sausages from portable hot water tanks. The sales pitch went something like this: "They're red-hot! Get your dachshund sausages while they're red-hot!"

As a sports cartoonist for the *New York Journal,* Dorgan took in the spectacle and conjured a caricature of barking dachshund sausages that were warm and comfortable in sandwich rolls. However, he didn't know how to spell "dachshund," so he wrote "hot dog!" instead. The cartoon was apparently so popular that the term "hot dog" entered the culinary lexicon.

The problem is, historians have never been able to dig up a copy of Dorgan's supposed "hot dog!" cartoon. And this has a lot of people shouting, "Bologna!" In fact, many experts, including recognized hot dog historian Bruce Kraig, say that the term "hot dog" was appearing in college magazines by the 1890s.

So maybe what makes a hot dog hot is not so much its temperature, but rather the amount of heated debate that surrounds it.

Q Did the Italians steal their spaghetti?

A Talk about a raw deal. Almost as soon as we learn to love spaghetti and any number of other pasta staples, we're told to hold up—the Italians didn't invent spaghetti. Innocence can end in a variety of ways, and for some of us, it's when we're told that pasta pitchers like Al Molinaro, of *Happy Days* and On-Cor commercial fame, have been lobbing us a lie.

The "untold story" usually centers on Marco Polo, the Italian explorer who filled a bag full of Eastern innovations and then sailed back to Venice in the late thirteenth century. While it's true that the Chinese made noodles for thousands of years before Italians had the bright idea of dribbling tomato sauce on them, Chinese noodles are made from rice, whereas spaghetti comes from wheat.

But those sly Italians aren't off the hook, because while they didn't steal pasta from the Chinese, they likely did pilfer it from their then-enemies to the south, the Arabs. Pastas that we consider Italian—such as spaghetti—were actually brought to the country by Arab conquerors in the mid-twelfth century. In fact, spaghetti can be traced through Aramaic writings all the way back to the fifth century; it's even mentioned in the Jerusalem Talmud, which indicates that spaghetti was present in ancient Jerusalem.

Arab pasta makers turned standard dumplings (imagine the gnocchi of today) into long, thin strands of spaghetti. Because it could be dried and stored for months or even years, spaghetti was a food innovation rivaling rice for flexibility and shelf life.

Never ones to sleep on a good idea, the Italians can at least be credited for the mass production of pasta. Italians built the first pasta-making factories in 1824, which makes them directly responsible for turning Wednesday into Prince Spaghetti Night.

Q Does food in a freezer really burn?

A Freezer burn isn't the same kind of scorch you get when you overbake cookies or char sausages; it's more a condition of severe dehydration. It happens when ice crystals and moisture evaporate from the surfaces of freezer-stored foods. We're talking discolored Delmonico steaks, parched peas and poultry, and frostbitten foods spotted with grayish-white fuzz.

It's definitely not pretty, but freezer burn doesn't render foods unsafe to eat. It's fine to cut away the dry spots, either before or after cooking—just be prepared to chow down on something with the texture and flavor of old English leather. But, hey, if you're hungry enough, you'll find a way to enjoy it.

To prevent freezer burn from happening in the first place, keep your freezer at zero degrees Fahrenheit (or lower) and avoid fluctuating temperatures. This means stop opening the freezer door to stare longingly at that forbidden gallon of Rocky Road.

Another tip: When wrapping foods for the freezer, get as much air out of the wrap as possible. Use those vacuum-sealed food bags that you see on TV infomercials. It's a worthy investment if you're freezing, say, a slab of wild Alaskan salmon or Kobe beef.

More frugal types can use regular old plastic freezer bags and a drinking straw. Put your food in the bag, stick the straw in one corner of the opening, and suck all the air out. Then pinch that zipper seal closed as fast as you can. After all, you don't want your food to get burned before you even cook it.

Q How can a bottle of olive oil be a virgin?

A Not only can olive oil be a virgin—it can be an extra virgin. How's that possible?

Well, first of all, you've got to get your mind out of the gutter and into a bowl of fresh mozzarella and tomato salad drizzled with Colavita, Bertolli, or Pompeian. Virgin olive oil isn't classified as "virgin" in a sexual context—but it is somewhat pure and unspoiled in its own way. Its "virginity" has to do with how it's produced.

The process begins with ripe olives that are harvested from carefully cultivated olive trees (which are usually from Italy, Spain, and Greece). A day or two later, these olives are taken to a mill, and giant stone wheels that weigh several tons crush them into a mash.

The olive mash is spread onto thin mats, which are stacked into a press. As the press applies several hundred pounds of pressure, water and olive oil begin to flow. The oil is collected and allowed to settle into huge vats. The water is separated out by centrifuge or decanting.

The oil obtained from this first pressing of the olives is called virgin olive oil, because it's pure and unprocessed. No high heat, chemicals, or further refining is allowed.

If this virgin oil happens to be deemed particularly excellent in taste, color, and aroma, it might be called extra virgin olive oil. But first it has to meet labeling standards. To earn the grade, extra virgin oil must contain less than 1 percent free oleic acid, or acidity.

Extra virgin olive oil—the premium variety of olive oil—is pale yellow to bright green in color with a noticeably fruity taste. EVOO—the nickname made famous by TV chef Rachael Ray—is best appreciated uncooked and drizzled on salads, vegetables, and crusty bread.

It's interesting to note that not all extra virgin olive oils taste the same. Like wines, they can vary dramatically in flavor depending on the type and quality of the fruits pressed, the weather during the growing season, the time of the harvest, and the region from which the olives originated. For instance, Spanish olive oil is typically fruity and nutty, while Italian olive oil is more herbal and grassy. Oils from Tuscany and the southern region of Italy sometimes even end on a peppery note.

So now that you know what constitutes a virgin olive oil, what's the difference between, say, EVOO and ordinary olive oil? In order to be fit for consumption, ordinary (lower-quality) olive oil has to be sent to a refinery. There it's mechanically, thermally, and/or chemically processed to provide color and taste. You could say it's been around the block.

Q Is black pudding good for dessert?

A Maybe if you're Dracula or a parasitic leech. Black pudding isn't a sweet, creamy, chocolaty custard made by Swiss Miss. In England, Ireland, and Scotland, it's part of a traditional full breakfast. So no, you probably wouldn't want to trade your slice of apple pie for a large-link sausage that is made with pig's blood.

In North America and other parts of the world, black pudding is known by a more conspicuous name: blood sausage. To make it, fresh pig's blood is combined with suet (that's the hard, white fat from the pig's kidneys and loins), breadcrumbs, oatmeal, and seasonings (usually black pepper, cayenne, mace, coriander, herbs, and onion). This mixture is cooked together, stuffed into sausage casings (that's a nice way of saying "intestines"), and lightly poached.

From whose twisted mind did this sanguinary side dish sprout? Many food historians think black pudding has its origins in ancient Greece. Homer's *Odyssey*, written around 800 BC, even makes poetic reference: "As when a man beside a great fire has filled a sausage with fat and blood and turns it this way and that and is very eager to get it quickly roasted..."

The oldest documented recipe for black pudding is attributed to *Apicius*, a collection of Roman cookery recipes from the first few centuries AD. In this version, the blood is mixed with chopped hard-boiled egg yolks, pine kernels, onions, and leeks.

It's likely that most black pudding recipes came from the economic need to make use of everything when a pig was butchered. In medieval Europe, even relatively poor families had a pig for the annual late-autumn slaughter. This is a possible reason why black pudding became a delicacy to be enjoyed on the feast days.

Today, black pudding can be purchased already prepared (no need to slaughter a pig in your own backyard) and can be enjoyed any time of year. It only requires a gentle reheating in the fry pan, grill, or oven. Serve it sliced alongside fried eggs and bacon for a traditional UK breakfast, or try a new-fangled gourmet rendition along the lines of black pudding with wild mushroom sauce.

However elegant the preparation, the thought of black pudding may still make you squeamish. In this case, you might opt for a white pudding instead. Similar to black pudding (but sans the plasma), this sausage is made with white meat (chicken or pork), fat, oatmeal, and seasonings. Just steer clear of the original recipe—very old versions of Scottish white pudding call for sheep brain as a binding agent.

Q Is there a killer sushi?

A If you're planning to have a dignitary from Japan over for dinner, there's one delicacy from his homeland you may want to avoid preparing: pufferfish.

The pufferfish, also known as blowfish or fugu, is a homely creature that, when threatened, inflates itself and displays protective spikes that are filled with tetrodotoxin, a neurotoxin that is about 1,200 times more deadly than cyanide. The average pufferfish has enough of it in its three-foot-long body to kill thirty people.

Believe it or not, pufferfish is served raw as sushi, after the tetrodotoxin has been removed. This is, however, an inexact science; about one hundred people die every year in Japan from pufferfish that have been improperly prepared. The initial symptom of pufferfish poisoning is paralysis of the lips and face, which can appear from ten minutes to several hours after ingestion. The cause of death is respiratory paralysis. There is no known antidote to tetrodotoxin, but the treatment of symptoms includes aggressive measures to keep the airways open.

Sushi chefs who want to work with pufferfish go through an intensive program of study at the Harmonious Fugu Association in Tokyo. They're taught how to prepare the creature for consumption, including how to cut and separate the toxic parts from the edible ones. Last, but certainly not least, they're taught first aid.

Why would someone eat pufferfish? Well, it's akin to mountain climbing, bungee jumping, or skydiving—the thrill of trying to cheat death. When a person at a sushi bar orders pufferfish, it is traditional to offer many toasts to his or her health. This person, this gastronomic renegade, becomes the center of attention.

While the pufferfish is an extreme example, sushi in general is a relatively high-risk food. Raw fish is full of bacteria, and mercury levels—particularly in tuna—have become an issue. The traditional accompaniments to sushi are meant to help. Vinegar is added to the rice to heighten the pH level and potentially kill bacteria; wasabi and pink pickled ginger also have bacteria-killing properties.

Nevertheless, you might want to consider introducing that Japanese dignitary to a dish called pizza.

Q Is white chocolate really chocolate?

A Let's say it's not. Would that make you love it any less? Didn't think so. But if we're going to get all technical with our candy confections, you should know that white chocolate is not a true chocolate, at least as defined by the U.S. Food and Drug Administration (FDA).

According to the FDA's standards of identity, a product called chocolate must contain chocolate liquor. White chocolate has none. So just what is this distinctive chocolate liquor? For starters, it's not alcohol.

To make chocolate, cocoa beans are harvested from the tropical *Theobroma cacao* tree. (The literal translation of this genus name is "food of the gods.") The beans are fermented, dried, roasted, and cracked to separate the nibs (which contain the good stuff) from the shells. The nibs are ground, and the resulting thick, dark paste is called chocolate liquor.

Chocolate liquor is what gives chocolate its intense bitter flavor and rich brown color. Unsweetened chocolate, or baking chocolate, is made from pure, hardened chocolate liquor, so it's very dark and bitter. By comparison, middle-of-the-road semisweet chocolate contains at least 35 percent chocolate liquor, and the light and mild milk chocolate has only a minimum of 10 percent chocolate liquor.

It's no wonder that white chocolate, with 0 percent chocolate liquor, has no real chocolaty flavor or pigment. Pure white to creamy yellow in color, it has more of a sweet, milky, creamy, dairy flavor—and that's fine with most of us.

White chocolate is typically made from a mixture of sugar, milk, lecithin (an emulsifier), vanilla, and cocoa butter. Cocoa butter is a natural, cream-colored vegetable fat that's extracted from cocoa beans during the chocolate-making process. It adds smoothness and flavor to chocolate and other foods.

But back to edible items: In 2004, the FDA gave white chocolate its due by establishing its own standard of identity. Any product that is labeled and marketed as white chocolate must contain at least 20 percent cocoa butter, 14 percent milk solids, and 3.5 percent milk fat, and not more than 55 percent sugar.

Why is this important? Because there are white chocolate imposters out there. Beware of any white chocolate that doesn't list cocoa butter on the ingredient label. Its quality and flavor is bound to be inferior, and you wouldn't want that in your next batch of white chocolate macadamia nut cookies.

Q Saccharin, Splenda, Equal— what's the difference?

A Let's throw in cyclamates, too. Are all of these artificial sweeteners the same? No. They differ in taste and strength, and possibly in their effect on the human body. But most of us can't keep them straight.

Saccharin was the first artificial sweetener that was discovered, back in 1879. Chemist Constantin Fahlberg, while working on coal-tar derivatives, went home from his lab at Johns Hopkins University with something on his hands that tasted sweet. After Fahlberg patented saccharin, his mentor asserted that he was the one who had spilled saccharin on Fahlberg's hands, but it didn't do him any good. Fahlberg kept the patent and the profits.

And there were profits. Although saccharin was banned briefly, starting in 1912, from foods in the United States because of questions about its wholesomeness, World War I caused sugar shortages and the ban was lifted. Saccharin sales took off. After decades of popularity, saccharin was banned again when it was removed from the government's list of safe substances in the 1970s. In 1977 the ban was replaced with a warning label about its potential dangers, and in 1996 Congress repealed the requisite warning notice on items that contain saccharin. However, saccharin has been banned in Canada since 1977.

Other sweeteners were discovered in much the same way: Scientists spilled things in their labs and realized the spills tasted sweet. In 1937, a graduate student at the University of Illinois discovered cyclamate when he picked up his cigarette from a lab bench. He'd been working on anti-fever drugs. In 1965, aspartame got on the fingertips of a chemist who was researching ulcer treatments for the G. D. Searle Company. In 1976, a London graduate student at King's College confused a request for "testing" as "tasting" and discovered sucralose while doing some work for Tate & Lyle, a sugar company.

We see the results of these discoveries every time we go into a coffee shop. The pink Sweet 'N Low packet is saccharin, the blue Equal is aspartame, and the yellow Splenda is sucralose.

The products are not equally sweet. Saccharin is three hundred times sweeter than sugar, and aspartame/Equal is 160 to two hundred times sweeter and lacks a bitter aftertaste. Sucralose/Splenda is six hundred times sweeter than sugar, so it is mixed with fiber to give it some volume.

And cyclamate? It's only thirty to forty times sweeter than sugar. Cyclamate, one of the original ingredients in Sweet 'N Low, was banned by the U.S. Food and Drug Administration after controversial tests linked the substance to cancer in lab rats. It is marketed in other countries as Sugar Twin. (In the United States, Sugar Twin is saccharin.)

Although tests on those pitiful lab rats frequently raise cancer scares, sugar-free products are big business. Nearly two hundred million Americans eat or drink sugar-free foods. Diet soda, for example, accounted for nearly 30 percent of all soft drink sales in

2007—and Americans spent about seventy billion dollars on soft drinks. Soda companies obviously don't need sugar in order for their sales to be sweet.

Q What is the shelf life of a Twinkie?

A Do Hostess Twinkies really have a shelf life of fifty years or more? If you were around during the Cold War in the 1950s and 1960s, when a nuclear attack from the Soviet Union seemed possible, you might believe they do.

Back then, Twinkies were a staple of the survival foods people stocked in household bomb shelters. This helped spawn the notion that the spongy snacks could withstand not only a nuclear holocaust, but also the ravages of time.

Truth is, a Twinkie's shelf life is twenty-five days. If even twenty-five days seems like a lot of stay-fresh time for a baked product, consider that Twinkies are a processed, packaged food and contain no dairy ingredients that can go bad in a hurry. Like many other commercially baked goods, they're tweaked with preservatives and stabilizing trans fats.

Check the label and you'll find such ingredients as vegetable and/or animal shortening and partially hydrogenated soybean, cottonseed, or canola oil. These artificially produced fats are more solid than clear liquid oils and, thus, are less likely to spoil. They help Twinkies stay soft and tasty, though not for years or decades.

The Cold War is history, but Twinkies are still plenty popular. Hostess bakers churn out one thousand per minute, which puts the kibosh on another urban legend: Due to an error in market research, the company overproduced Twinkles two decades ago, hasn't made any since, and will not resume production until all the "vintage Twinkles" are eaten.

Chapter Seven

PLACES

Q Why won't men ask for directions?

A Everyone's heard the old joke that asks, "Why does it take one hundred million sperm to fertilize one egg?" Answer: "Because none of them will stop for directions."

The stereotype that men refuse to ask for directions has been fertile territory for amateur comedians over the years; at the same time, experience seems to suggest that there may be some truth to it. In fact, we suspect plenty of women—perhaps some who are reading this right now, as they are being driven farther and farther away from their destinations by men who insist they are not lost—are eagerly awaiting the answer to this question.

Though it might be small consolation, researchers have claimed to have evidence that suggests men's disinclination to ask for directions may be because they have a better chance of not getting lost in the first place. According to a 2000 study in *Nature Neuroscience,* men might have trouble asking for directions simply because they are naturally better than women at finding their way around. The study, which examined men's and women's brain responses to spatial puzzles, found that the left hippocampal region—the part of the brain involved in spatial problems—activated more frequently and intensely in men than in women. Accordingly, men were consistently better than women at solving spatial and directional puzzles. The study posits that men use more geometric or spatial cues to find their way, while women tend to use landmarks. (Which helps explain why women more frequently say, "Go left at the McDonald's," while men tend to say, "Head east on Main Street" when providing directions.)

How did this develop? For the answer, we look to socio-biologists, evolutionary experts who attempt to explain biological traits based on evolutionary theory; in particular, natural selection. According to socio-biologists, men developed better neural compasses because way back in their chest-beating, club-wielding caveman days, males foraged far and wide for food for their families, while females stayed in the caves, tending to the youngsters. Better foragers—with a better sense of direction—not only had increased chances of survival, but also proved more attractive as potential mates; thus, the genes for "direction" were passed on.

So, ladies, the next time your husband claims that he's not lost, give him a break. There's a chance he just can't help it. Now, if only those socio-biologists could figure out why men can't put the toilet seat down.

Q Where is Oz?

A What, doesn't everyone know that Oz is somewhere over the rainbow? Is there a soul in the civilized world who hasn't traveled with Dorothy and Toto to that magical kingdom that was brought to life in the 1939 classic *The Wizard of Oz?* The young Dorothy (Judy Garland) and her beloved dog are whisked off their Kansas chicken ranch by that tornado and ultimately follow the Yellow Brick Road to Oz, where they meet the mighty wizard.

Beyond the fantasy, though, why not pin down the actual physical location of Oz? Impossible, you say? No, indeed. First of all, we can rule out one state because Dorothy utters the famous line, "Toto, I've a feeling we're not in Kansas anymore."

So where could the tornado have tossed Dorothy and her pooch? Well, even assuming this was one of the most devastating twisters of all time—an F5 on the Fujita scale used by meteorologists—there's a limit to how far a human being can be carried by a tornado. According to researchers at the Tornado Project in St. Johnsbury, Vermont, small objects have whooshed great distances, but the farthest a human being has been thrown is about one mile.

So Dorothy couldn't have gone far—let's say a mile and a half because she was smaller than a full-grown adult. Therefore, Dorothy must have lived right on the Kansas border. And not out in the middle of nowhere, either, because at the start of the film, farm worker Hickory makes this statement: "But someday, they're going to erect a statue to me in this town."

So liftoff was near some kind of city or village right at the edge of Kansas. And you have to assume that Oz itself couldn't have been in an empty cornfield, either, because there would have needed to be some sort of population where Dorothy and Toto landed. Only the northern and eastern borders of Kansas provide search points, because most tornadoes move from southwest to northeast. A twister on either of the state's other two borders would have carried Dorothy and Toto further into Kansas.

There is only one location that fits the description provided in the movie. Dorothy's Uncle Henry and Aunt Em must have lived just outside of Atchison, Kansas—east of Highway 7 near the Missouri River—and the infamous tornado carried girl and dog little more than a mile to the outskirts of Rushville, Missouri. Oz.

Before you scoff, consider some curious coincidences. Tornado activity in the Rushville area is 143 percent greater than the overall U.S. average. Oh, and Atchison is the birthplace of Amelia Earhart. The gallant aviatrix, Atchison's most famous daughter if you aren't counting Dorothy, vanished on her flight around the world in 1937 but was declared dead in 1939—the same year *The Wizard of Oz* was released. Perhaps Amelia can be found over the rainbow.

Q Why is Australia considered a continent instead of an island?

A In grammar school, some of us were far more interested in the "social" aspect of social studies than the "studies" part. Nevertheless, everyone can recite the continents: Africa,

Asia, Europe, South America, North America, Australia, and... some other one. What gives with Australia? Why is it a continent? Shouldn't it be an island?

It most certainly is an island (the world's largest) and so much more. Australia is the only land mass on Earth to be considered an island, a country, and a continent.

Australia is by far the smallest continent, leading one to wonder why it is labeled a continent at all when other large islands, such as Greenland, are not. The answer lies in plate tectonics, the geologic theory explaining how Earth's land masses got to where they are today. According to plate tectonic theory, all of Earth's continents once formed a giant land mass known as Pangaea. Though Pangaea was one mass, it actually comprised several distinct pieces of land known as plates.

Over millions of years, at roughly the speed of your hair growth, these plates shifted, drifting apart from one another until they reached their current positions. Some plates stayed connected, such as South America and North America, while others moved off into a remote corner like a punished child, such as Australia. (It's no wonder Australia was first used by the British as a prison colony.) Because Australia is one of these plates—while Greenland is part of the North American plate—it gets the honor of being called a continent.

All of this debate might ultimately seem rather silly. Some geologists maintain that in 250 million years, the continents will move back into one large mass called Pangaea Ultima. Australia will merge with Southeast Asia—and social studies tests will get a whole lot easier.

Q Why does it take longer to fly west than east?

A If you've ever flown a long distance, you might have noticed that it takes more time to fly from east to west than west to east. As Seinfeld might say, "What's the deal with that?" Since there's no real traffic in the sky (apart from the occasional flock of birds), the delay seems inexplicable. It should take the same amount of time, regardless of direction.

But the bitter truth is, the air up there isn't quite as wide open as it seems. At the high altitude that is required for commercial flights, there's a powerful and persistent horizontal wind known as the jet stream. Because of the differences in temperature and pressure between the equator and the earth's polar regions, the jet stream flows from west to east in the Northern Hemisphere. This jet stream is a lot like a current in a river: If you're moving with the current, you'll go faster; conversely, working against the current slows you down and makes you work harder to get where you're going.

The airlines, of course, know all about the wily ways of the jet stream. They take advantage of it, purposely flying within it on eastbound flights to allow planes to reach their destinations sooner and with less wear and tear. (Some airlines even offer cheaper fares on the eastbound leg of a journey.) But on a westbound flight, a pilot must fly against the jet stream, which obviously means that it takes more time.

A westerly cross-country flight lasts about a half-hour longer than its easterly counterpart. Though it's invisible to the naked eye, the jet stream is like a giant traffic jam in the sky.

Q Why are Poland natives called Poles, but Holland natives aren't called Holes?

A Have you ever heard the phrase *pars pro toto?* Don't worry if you haven't—it's not exactly something that would come up during your dinner conversation. It's Latin for "a part for the whole." When talking geography, this refers to the practice of using a small part of a country to describe the whole country (or a larger area). For instance, many people refer to the United Kingdom as England, when in reality the United Kingdom consists of England, Scotland, Wales, and Northern Ireland.

Why are we mentioning this string of words in a dead language? Because Holland is a perfect example of *pars pro toto.* When people talk about Holland, they're most often referring to the country called The Netherlands. Holland is a western part of The Netherlands that consists of two provinces, North Holland and South Holland. It's kind of like if you were to call the United States New England or the Southwest.

That's all well and good, but it still doesn't explain why we don't call people from Holland "Holes," so let's explain it now. First off, Holland does not sound the same as Poland. Poland is pronounced Pole-and, but Holland is not pronounced Hole-and. So it's a bit lazy to use "Hole" as a shorthand.

But "it sounds wrong" isn't the only reason "Hole" isn't used. See, Pole comes from a Polish word that means "field dwellers," and there's no comparable description for Holes. Not only that, English-speaking people often refer to folks from The Netherlands as Dutch. The word "Dutch" first popped up in the fourteenth century, and it came from the German word for the Germanic people, *Deutsch.* By the sixteenth century, Dutch referred to anyone who spoke a Germanic language. (English people in the Middle Ages weren't the most sensitive bunch.) Over the years, Dutch and German eventually came to mean what they do today. So to many English speakers, anyone from Holland is simply Dutch. People from The Netherlands, however, usually refer to themselves as Nederlanders.

It's interesting to note that the name Holland, rather than The Netherlands, is often used to promote the country because it's the term that's more recognized around the world. Holland is also used by some Dutch people informally, though there are areas in which calling someone a Hollander is an insult. Oh, and they don't all wear wooden clogs and pick flowers in front of windmills. But that would be lovely, wouldn't it?

Q Which genius thought Rhode Island was an island?

A The history of exploration is, in some ways, a history of mistakes. Ponce de Leon blundered through the swamps of Florida because he believed that he was going to find the Fountain of Youth. Ferdinand Magellan believed that it would take only three days to sail from South America to Indonesia (try four months). And, of course, Christopher Columbus was so confused as to believe that a tiny island in the Caribbean was India.

To some extent, these mistakes are understandable—no European had been to the Caribbean previously—but others, not so much. For example, it would take a geographically challenged individual of the highest order to believe that a body of land bordered on only one side by water should be called an island. Yet that's precisely what the founders of Rhode Island seem to have done.

A quick glance at the map will tell you that islands do make up a chunk of Rhode Island's decidedly small landmass, though the vast majority of it lies on the continent, wedged between Massachusetts and Connecticut. And a quick glance at the Constitution will tell you that Rhode Island isn't the official name of the state at all. The official name is "The State of Rhode Island and Providence Plantations." How Rhode Island got that name is almost as confusing as how a body of land the size of a postage stamp can be legitimately termed a state in the first place.

This whole mess may be the result of a misunderstanding. Some historians argue that Rhode Island was named by confused settlers who believed that they were living on a body of land that the sixteenth-century explorer Giovanni da Verrazzano likened to the Mediterranean Greek island of Rhodes; hence, they began calling their home Rhode Island. The only problem is that the island about which Verrazzano had waxed classical was a different island—the one that is now called Block Island.

The official story, though, is that Rhode Island got its name from the Dutch explorer Adriaen Block—he whose namesake island should actually be called Rhode—who called the region *Roodt Eylandt* ("Red Island") after the color of the local clay. When British settlers moved in, they anglicized the name to Rhode Island.

In 1636, Roger Williams, after being kicked out of the Massachusetts Bay Colony, founded his own settlement on the mainland beside Narragansett Bay. He named it Providence in the belief that divine intervention had led him there. Williams, a theologian who advocated tolerance and free thinking (neither of which had any place in the Massachusetts Bay Colony), eventually convinced settlers of the bay's islands—which included Rhode—to join him. The eventual State of Rhode Island and Providence Plantations was born, later shortened to Rhode Island by lazy Americans.

Despite the series of blunders that led to its name, Rhode Island forged and maintains a reputation for culture and tolerance. The state was one of the first to pass laws banning slavery and one of only two that currently has laws allowing prostitution. Fourteen colleges and universities are crammed into its borders, and the Ivy League's Brown University is considered one of the finest educational institutions in the world. Its geography department, however, must be considered suspect.

Q Is the North Star always in the north?

A The answer is yes, but it's not quite that simple. Although the North Star is always in the north, it isn't always the same star.

The North Star is also called the Pole Star because it is the star most directly above Earth's North Pole. It appears due north of the observer, and the angle between it and the horizon tells the latitude of the observer. Consequently, the North Star has been used for navigation for thousands of years.

However, the North Star has limited capability as a navigational tool. Because it is only visible in the Northern Hemisphere, it is of no help south of the equator. There is no precise Southern Hemisphere equivalent to the North Star, although the constellation Crux, or the Southern Cross, points to the South Pole.

But back to the North Star and why its identity changes: Due to the precession of the equinoxes (which is a fancy astronomer's term for "the Earth wobbles when it turns"), the axis upon which our planet rotates shifts ever so slightly. As the shift occurs over many centuries, another star in the distance elbows its way in as the useful North Star. Currently, it's Polaris, a middling bright star at the end of the Little Dipper's handle, about 430 light years from Earth.

Time is running out for Polaris, just as it did for its predecessors. In 3000 BC, the star Thuban in the constellation Draco served as the North Star. In AD 3000, Gamma Cephei, or Alrai, will get the call. Iota Cephei will have its turn in AD 5200, followed by Vega in AD 14000.

For now, though, Polaris will guide you if you are lost. Unless you happen to be adrift off the coast of, say, Peru. Then you're pretty much screwed.

Q If lightning terrifies you, where in the world should you avoid?

A Lightning frightens plenty of people, as Shakespeare pointed out in *King Lear:* "To stand against the deep dread-bolted thunder?/In the most terrible and nimble stroke/Of quick, cross lightning?"

Statistics provided by Britain's Royal Aeronautical Society back up the bard's fear. There are about twenty-four thousand lightning fatalities worldwide each year. In the United States alone, the National Weather Service reports that since 1959, nearly four thousand people have died and at least sixteen thousand have been injured from lightning strikes.

What can you do to avoid becoming one of these statistics? Well, don't play golf or soccer, for a start. Participants in those two sports are in particular danger because they're out in open fields. Multiple-death incidents have been reported on soccer pitches in Malawi, Indonesia, Malaysia, Colombia, Honduras, and Guatemala since 1993. Other lightning-avoidance strategies include not hanging around outdoors in threatening weather and staying off your landline telephone. Landline phone use is the leading cause of indoor lightning injuries in the United States—but it's safe to use a cordless phone or a cell phone.

And for your next family vacation, find a locale that is light on lightning. Since lightning is produced by the collision of hot and cold air, the ideal spot has a basically steady climate. Find a spot without wild weather extremes, either someplace cool year-round (like eastern Russia, northern and western Canada, or Alaska) or consistently warm and mild (Hawaii, if you can afford it). Alaska and Hawaii are the only states that haven't had a lightning fatality since 1959.

Then there are the spots to avoid, starting with central Africa. According to *Extreme Weather: A Guide and Record Book,* there are eight places in the world that endure more than two hundred thunderstorm days per year, and six are in central Africa. Kamembe, Rwanda, in east-central Africa, is third on this dubious list, with an average of 221 thunderstorm days. According to the National Lightning Safety Institute, Kamembe endures an incredible 82.7 lightning strikes per square kilometer each year, an average of sixteen more strikes than any other area in the world.

In the United States, don't rush to these general areas, according to the authors of *Extreme Weather*: the Gulf Coast, the Florida peninsula, and the peak of the front range of the Rocky Mountains. Florida easily tops all states in lightning deaths, with an average of ten per year.

Don't linger out in the countryside; urban centers are safer. Authorities attribute the significant decrease in lightning-related deaths and injuries in the United States since 1900 to the country's mass migration from rural areas to the cities.

As for Shakespeare and lightning, he was pretty darned safe, despite what he wrote. Britain's Met Office notes that the country averages three lightning deaths per year. That's one per twenty million residents—among the lowest rates in the world.

Q How many people live at the North Pole besides Santa and his elves?

A The population at the North Pole is as transient as the terrain itself, which is in a constant state of flux due to shifting and melting ice. Human life in this frigid region consists of researchers floating on makeshift stations and tourists who aren't the sit-on-a-beach-in-the-Bahamas type. There are no permanent residents at the North Pole—save, of course, for Santa Claus and his posse.

When you're talking about the North Pole, you're referring to four different locales: geographic, magnetic, geomagnetic, and the pole of inaccessibility. The geographic North Pole, known as true north or ninety degrees north, is where all longitudinal lines converge. It sits roughly four hundred and fifty miles north of Greenland, in the center of the Arctic Ocean. The magnetic pole—the point marker for compasses—is located about one hundred miles south of the geographic pole, northwest of the Queen Elizabeth Islands, which are part of northern Canada. Its position moves about twenty-five miles annually. In fact, the magnetic pole has drifted hundreds of miles from its point of discovery in 1831. Then there's the North Geomagnetic Pole, the northern end of the axis of the magnetosphere, the geomagnetic field that surrounds the earth and extends into space. Last is the Northern Pole of Inaccessibility, the point in the Arctic Ocean that is most distant from any landmass.

If the North Pole were more like its counterpart on the other end of the earth, the South Pole, it would be a lot more accessible. Since the South Pole is located on a continent, Antarctica, permanent settlements can be established. In fact, research stations at the South Pole have been in place since 1956. These bases range in population size, but most average fifteen personnel in winter (April to November) and one hundred and fifty in summer (December to March). Combined, the stations house a few thousand people in the summer. The U.S. McMurdo Station alone might exceed a thousand individuals at the peak time of year.

All of this helps explain why Santa chose to live at the North Pole rather than the South Pole. If you're S. Claus and you don't want to be found, there isn't a better place than the North Pole to set up shop, even if that shop is always in danger of floating away.

Q Do animals still get stuck in the La Brea Tar Pits?

A Yes, animals still get stuck in the La Brea Tar Pits. They're much smaller than they used to be, though. None of your saber-toothed cats or woolly mammoths—we're talking lizards and birds, mostly.

Tar pits are created when crude oil seeps through a fissure in the earth's crust. When oil hits the surface, the less dense elements of the oil evaporate, leaving behind a gooey, sticky substance known as asphalt, or tar.

La Brea is a Spanish name that translates literally to "the tar." These famous pits are located in Hancock Park in Los Angeles; they constitute the only active archeological excavation site to be situated in a major metropolitan area. The pits are tended by staff members of the George C. Page Museum, which is nearby. It is at the museum that the fossils currently being excavated from the pits are cleaned and examined.

Not only do the staff members get to parse through the well-preserved remnants of prehistory, but they also sometimes witness the natural process by which these remnants are preserved. An average of ten animals every thirty years get trapped in the pits.

The tar pits work like a large-scale glue trap. If an animal lets just one paw hit the surface of the asphalt, it sticks (especially on warm days, when the asphalt is at its stickiest). In its frenzy to free itself, the animal gets more stuck. Eventually, its nose and mouth will be covered, and then it's all over—just one more carcass for scientists to excavate.

The La Brea Tar Pits are forty thousand years old. Since the early twentieth century, scientists have uncovered the remains of 624 different species of plants and animals there. Because of the preservative qualities of the tar, and because most of the skeletons are complete, the discoveries from the tar pits have made La Brea an indispensable resource for the scientific community.

As for the animals that get stuck in the pits? They're not as lucky.

Chapter Eight

WEIRD SCIENCE AND TECHNOLOGY

Q Was the original computer bug literally a bug?

A The Mark II Aiken Relay Calculator was built at Harvard University for the U.S. Navy just after World War II. The Mark II wasn't a calculator like we know them today—it was a primitive computer, one of those comically giant, room-filling monstrosities that featured endless wires, switches, and relays. Today you see the Mark II in history books, with serious-looking technicians in lab coats posed in front of it.

One September day in 1947, the Mark II wasn't working properly. Computer operators investigated and found the problem on Panel F: A dead moth was gumming up relay number 70. The moth was removed and taped to the operator's log. The following words were written on the log beneath the moth: "First actual case of bug being found."

The Mark II moth has since gained some fame and is now enshrined at the National Museum of American History in Washington, D.C. It sometimes is referred to as the inspiration for the term "bug," and some people believe that it was the cause of the first-ever computer bug. Both claims are nonsense, of course.

The fact that the operators recognized the joke—that an actual bug was the "bug" in their computer system—suggests that the term already existed. And indeed it did. The term had been used to describe glitches in mechanics and electronics for many years. The *Oxford English Dictionary* traces its use back to 1889, in a published account of Thomas Edison working on "a bug" in his phonograph.

And it certainly wasn't the first time someone had a problem with a computer. You think your PC gives you headaches? There's a reason why none of those technicians in lab coats were smiling.

Q Why do speedometers list speeds faster than you can legally drive?

A Zip along a stretch of rural Texas Interstate at eighty miles per hour and you'll be driving just about as fast as you can go anywhere in our speed-craving country without risking a ticket. But unless you're driving some kind of Yugoslavian relic, you'll still have plenty of room to inch that needle higher on your car's speedometer. Let's say your ride is a 505-horsepower Chevrolet Corvette Z06—you'll have a whopping 120 miles per hour of speed-gauge breathing room. Is Chevy begging us to break the law? Is the company all but telling us to slam the gas pedal to the floor?

Ask experts why automakers install speedometers that mock posted limits—which usually range from sixty-five to eighty miles per hour on the highway, depending on the state you're in—and you will get discussions of manufacturing efficiencies, hints of subliminal messages, and psychological explanations that offer something in between.

"It's a one-word answer: testosterone," says Alex Fedorak, a veteran of more than two decades in car-company public relations. "It's a guy thing. They want to think they can do it, even if they never do."

Less sanguine is Richard Retting, senior transportation engineer with the Insurance Institute for Highway Safety, an underwriter-industry lobbying group. "There's no reason for any car to have a speedometer that goes over eighty miles per hour because there's no place in this country you can legally drive faster than that," Retting says. "Why car speedometers go up to 120 or 140 miles per hour makes no sense—except for marketing.

"It's no secret that speed is a key strategy for marketing vehicles in this country. Someone who bought a high-horsepower, high-speed car presumably would not be happy with a speedometer that gave the impression the car would not go up to that speed, even if they never approached that speed."

Automakers cite the economic efficiency of producing a single speedometer that's good in several countries, in which speed limits may be higher or in kilometers per hour. General Motors, which builds cars for use in virtually every nation on earth, requires its speedometers to indicate true vehicle speed at all times and to reflect the top speed of the fastest-rated tire that can be used on a particular vehicle.

Betwixt talk of testosterone and tires lies the nuanced approach of Stuart Norris, who is responsible for GM's global instrument design strategies, Norris acknowledges issues of engineering and standardization, but he also waxes about speedometer aesthetics, about the way the numerals are distributed on the speedometer's face, and how large, elegant type sends one message (luxury) and starker, closely spaced markings another (sporty). And all this time, we thought a speedometer simply indicated how fast you were going. Who knew there's much more to it than that?

A speedometer that ended at, say, eighty-five miles per hour, would "look under-populated, half-baked, even childlike," Norris says. "There's a premium-ness associated with a more populated gauge." As for that final numeral, "On a vehicle that's rated for 155 miles per hour, we expect the gauge to indicate the capability of the vehicle, even though we don't expect the customer to drive that speed."

In the end, it's all about ego. A speedometer that goes up to two hundred miles per hours connotes power, even if you can never fully unleash that power.

Q Did Ben Franklin really discover electricity?

A If by "discover," we mean to ask if Ben Franklin was the first to stumble upon electricity, the answer is no. But there's more to the story.

The ancient Greeks knew about static electricity. They observed amber, which they called *elektron,* drawing feathers and twigs to itself when rubbed with a cloth. Static electricity remained an amusing trick until the eighteenth century, when an Englishman named Stephen Gray found that electricity could be "sent" hundreds of feet if the right material was used to conduct it. Dutch professor Pieter van Musschenbroek of Leyden figured out that electricity could be stored in water-filled jars. He realized this after he touched a wire that was sticking out of a jar and accidentally electrocuted himself. He survived, and Leyden jars became the rage among scientists.

News of Leyden jars and electrical displays eventually reached the intellectual backwater of North America, where wealthy printer Ben Franklin saw a demonstration and became fascinated. He ordered jars and scientific journals from London and set up his own experiments.

Here's where it gets a bit tricky. There's a second definition of "discover": to obtain knowledge of something through study. In this sense, Franklin did indeed discover a lot about electricity. Tricks aside, he was determined to find a real, practical use for the strange energy. In pursuit of this audacious goal, Franklin was knocked senseless while arranging to use electricity to kill and roast a turkey.

Like other scientists, Franklin suspected that lightning was pure electricity. Two years after his accident, Franklin and his son launched a specially built silk kite into a stormy sky. The kite was not, in fact, struck by lightning. By simply remaining airborne under storm clouds the kite was electrified—and so was the metal key that was tied to its tail near Franklin's hand.

It seems simple now, but figuring out a way to prove that lightning was electricity made Franklin famous on both sides of the Atlantic. Franklin, while still in his forties, received honorary degrees from Harvard and Yale and a gold medal from London's Royal Society. He was a celebrity—and the American Revolution hadn't even started.

Q How does glow-in-the-dark stuff work?

A Switch off the light in the bedroom of a typical eight-year-old and you might see a ceiling glowing with stars, planets, and dinosaurs. "'Tis vile witchcraft!" you may shout, reaching around for some rope and a torch. Wait! Before you burn the kid at the stake, let's review simple physics.

Atoms gain and lose energy through the movement of electrons. Electrons are the tiny, negatively charged particles that orbit the atom's positively charged nucleus. When something energizes an atom, an electron jumps from a lower orbital (closer to the atom's nucleus) to a higher orbital (farther from the atom's nucleus). Basically, the atom is storing energy that will be released in some form when the electron falls back to the lower orbital.

Light is one thing that can energize an atom in this way. When a light photon (an individual packet of light energy) hits the atom, that energy boosts an electron to a higher orbital. Some atoms can release energy as light: When the electron falls back to a lower orbital, the stored extra energy is emitted as a light photon.

Glow-in-the-dark stuff contains atoms that do just this; they're called phosphors. When you turn on the lights in your kid's room, the photons from the light excite these atoms and boost their electrons to higher orbitals. When you turn off the lights, the atoms release the stored energy. The electrons return to a lower level, emit photons, and the atoms glow. There's some energy loss in the process, so the glowing light of the little dinosaur will be of a different frequency (a different color) than the light that excited the atom in the first place.

Phosphors are everywhere. Your fingernails, teeth, and bodily fluids all contain natural phosphors. Your white clothes are phosphorescent too, thanks to whitening agents in laundry detergent. This is why all this stuff glows under a black light. The black light emits invisible ultraviolet light, which causes the phosphors to glow. (Dark clothes may contain the phosphor, too, but the dark pigments absorb the UV light.)

Most phosphors have very short persistence—the atoms release the light energy immediately after they're charged, so they glow only when light is shining on them. By contrast, glow-in-the-dark stickers and the like are made of phosphors such as zinc sulfide and strontium aluminate that have unusually long persistence, so they keep glowing after you turn out the lights. Manufacturers mix these phosphors with plastic to make glow-in-the dark items in many shapes and sizes.

Other types of phosphors react to radiation from radioactive elements and compounds rather than from visible light radiation. This is how the hands on some watches glow with no charging required: They're coated with a radioactive isotope of hydrogen called tritium or promethium that's mixed with phosphors.

As you now know, there's a scientific explanation for glowing stars on the bedroom ceiling. So you can put away the rope and the torch.

Q What is the Vomit Comet?

A Actually, it's an airplane, any one of several owned by NASA and used over the past fifty years to train astronauts and conduct experiments in a zero-gravity environment.

The plane simulates the absence of gravity by flying in a series of parabolas—arcs that resemble the path of an especially gut-wrenching roller coaster. When the Vomit Comet descends toward the earth, its passengers experience weightlessness for the twenty to twenty-five seconds it takes to reach the bottom of the parabola. Then the plane flies back up to repeat the maneuver, beginning a new dive from an altitude of over thirty thousand feet.

Being weightless and buoyant might bring on nausea all by itself, but when the plane arcs, dips, and ascend again, the riders feel about twice as heavy as usual. The wild ride induces many of its otherwise steely-stomached passengers to vomit—hence, the name. (The plane is also called, by those with a greater sense of propriety, the Weightless Wonder.)

NASA has used the Vomit Comet to train astronauts for the Mercury, Gemini, Apollo, Skylab, Space Shuttle, and Space Station programs. The first Vomit Comets, which were unveiled in 1959 as part of the Mercury program, were C-131 Samaritans. A series of KC-135A Stratotankers came next. The most famous of these, the NASA 930, was retired in 1995 after twenty-two years of service as NASA's primary reduced-gravity research plane. This is the aircraft that was used to film the scenes of space weightlessness in the 1995 movie *Apollo 13*. It is now on public display at Ellington Field, near Johnson Space Center in Houston.

After the 930 was put out to pasture, another KC-135A took over, the NASA 931, which was retired in 2004. The 931 flew 34,757 parabolas, generating some 285 gallons of vomit. Yes, the engineers at NASA measured the barf. Since 2005, a C-9—the military version of the DC-9 aircraft produced by McDonnell Douglas—has been used to give astronauts a taste of weightlessness... and of bile.

Q Why can't you use cell phones in hospitals?

A It's no secret that we are a society that has become increasingly tethered to our cell phones. From texting to Twitter, we just love to update our friends and family about every little thing we do. Indeed, it's hard to believe that civilization flourished before such a technology existed. Can you imagine how much better the Renaissance would have been if Da Vinci had only known what Michelangelo was having for breakfast? And Einstein certainly would have completed his unified field theory if he had been kept apprised of Heisenberg's bathroom schedule.

Yet for all of today's obsession with instantly relaying the minutiae of our daily lives, we are completely cut off when we're at the one place in the world where such communication might be a necessity: the hospital. That's because many hospitals don't allow cell phones.

The problem lies in how cell phones operate. Cell phones use something called radiofrequency (RF) energy to send information through the air. RF energy is also used by microwaves, radars, television signals, and—to hospital officials' concern—medical devices such as pacemakers and patient-monitoring systems. Fear that cell phone signals might wreak electromagnetic havoc on important medical equipment has led many hospitals to err on the side of caution and ban cell phones.

However, there's an ongoing debate about whether banning cell phones in hospitals is wise. Part of the issue is that studies repeatedly contradict each other regarding cell phone dangers to hospital equipment. In 2006, a study released by the Yale School of Medicine found that the benefits of improved communication via cell phones outweighed the minuscule odds of complications caused by electromagnetic interference. In 2007, the Mayo Clinic published the findings of a five-month study that showed cell phone usage did not interfere with patient-care equipment; the report argued that the hospitals ban on cell phones should be reconsidered.

But six months later, a Dutch research team that was examining the effects of cell phones found that there was a significant risk—twenty-six of the sixty-one medical devices it tested were disrupted when cell phones were used close by. Critics were quick to point out that in the Dutch study the researchers tested the medical devices with replicated cell phone signals, not actual cell phones, and tested them at intensities that were several times more powerful than the average cell phone.

Most hospitals are starting to lean toward relaxing the ban, or at least toward maintaining it only in surgical and intensive care units. This shouldn't come as much of a surprise. After more than a decade of cell phone ubiquity, evidence of incidents caused by cell phone use in hospital settings is anecdotal at best. Indeed, there have been more verified cases of people's pacemakers going haywire due to retail stores' antitheft devices than from cell phone frequencies.

So have faith, all you members of the IM generation: It probably won't be long before your friends, family, and coworkers can hear about your stool sample in real time.

Q Why do boats float?

A Imagine Bob hopping into a nice hot bath, only to watch helplessly as the water spills over the edge. He filled it up to a decent level a moment ago, so what happened? Bob happened. He displaced the water, taking its place and leaving it with nowhere to go but up and over. Displacement is a really important factor in making things float, so let's leave Bob and his poor bathing skills behind and focus on an ancient Greek guy named Archimedes.

Archimedes came up with the principle of buoyancy (in other words, an explanation of why stuff floats). After an incident similar to Bob's, Archimedes realized that objects in water experience an upward force. That upward force is equal to the weight of the water that the object displaces. If the displaced water weighs the same as the object, the object will float. Say the object is Bob. If he's swimming in the sea and displaces two hundred pounds of water, and he weighs 220 pounds, he's going to sink to the bottom. If he displaces two hundred pounds of water and weighs two hundred pounds, then he's going to float.

So obviously, boats weigh exactly the same amount as the water that they displace, and therefore they can float merrily along. But wait—Bob's looking very confused. He's probably thinking, "Boats are basically big pieces of solid steel. If I dropped a big piece of solid steel into water, it'd just sink. I smell a rat." It's true—boats are pretty heavy. The biggest boat in the world right now is the *Knock Nevis,* which is 1,504 feet long, displaces almost 648,000 tons of water when fully loaded, and has a "draft" of eighty-one feet (meaning the very bottom of it is eighty-one feet under water). Why doesn't it sink like a stone?

The key here is density—the amount of weight in a certain volume. For instance, a small stone is fairly dense, but a piece of cork that weighs the same as the stone is spread out over a larger volume. Because the stone is smaller, it displaces less water and sinks. But the cork displaces more water than the stone because of its larger volume, so it floats.

Boats are not as dense as you might think. Sure, they're made of steel, but that's only their outer bits. Inside, they've got a bunch of air floating around in space. The air doesn't add to their weights; but it does add to their volume, so they're like the cork: Their weights are spread out over large areas. They're shaped like they are because "boat-shaped" is good for spreading that weight around as large an area as possible. And because that weight covers such a large area, the boat is able to displace the same amount of water as its weight and—that's right—float.

As for Bob, let's just hope that he puts a little less water in the tub next time and avoids any spillage. Water, after all, is a precious resource.

Q Why do traffic lights use the colors red, yellow, and green?

A This is reminiscent of a question you might find on a driver's education test in high school: "What do the colors of a traffic light indicate?" The answer: "Red equals stop, green equals go, and yellow equals slam on the gas." But why red, yellow, and green? Why not purple, pink, and blue?

For the answer, we need to look at the history of traffic signals. The first traffic light was for pedestrians, not vehicles. In 1868, outside the British House of Parliament, a railroad employee named J. P. Knight installed a gas-powered two-light signal. Being a railroad man, J. P. borrowed the signaling pattern used for train traffic: Red meant stop, and green meant proceed with caution. Unfortunately, the machinery was somewhat limited, as it had to be operated by hand. It also had a tendency to explode, which it did rather dramatically barely three weeks after being put into operation, killing the constable manning it.

It was more than four decades before traffic lights were given another shot, in the USA. With the Ford Motor Company putting a car in every driveway, the nation's roads were becoming a free-for-all. In 1914, tired of watching maniacs driving recklessly through Cleveland streets, the city fathers had an electric traffic light installed on Euclid Avenue, a street we can assume everyone started avoiding. This light used the same red-green system as the exploding British traffic signal; it wasn't until 1920 that a Detroit policeman thought of putting a yellow light between the red and green to indicate the lights were changing.

Why did that original pedestrian signal have red and green to symbolize stop and go? The colors were already the norm in the electrical industry, but how that choice was made in the first place is lost to history. Some color theorists surmise that red is traditionally associated with danger (think blood and fire), while green is linked to pleasing emotions (think spring). However, these same theorists claim that yellow denotes health and happiness. Funny—we would have thought haste and hurry.

Q How do they decaffeinate a coffee bean?

A We've seen seedless watermelon, fat-free chocolate, and Emmy nominations for Charlie Sheen. Here's further proof that anything is possible: the naturally caffeine-free coffee bean.

Stop and read that again—not decaf coffee, but an all-natural, no-processing-necessary decaf coffee bean, straight from the plant. Scientists reported in 2004 that they had found three coffee plants growing in Ethiopia that contained almost no caffeine. And they hope that by the end of the decade, they will be able to develop a market-ready breed from caffeine-free coffee plants —meaning it won't be too long before you're pouring yourself a warm cup of natural decaf.

Until then, you'll have to drink coffee that's been decaffeinated the old-fashioned way. Which raises the question: How do they remove caffeine from a coffee bean?

First, let's cover the basics. Decaffeinated coffee is at least 97 percent caffeine-free. When decaf was introduced in 1903, benzene was used in the caffeine-removal process. Yes, the same benzene that is a fuel additive and a known carcinogen. But fear not—this technique is a thing of the past. Contemporary caffeine-removal methods, called direct extraction and indirect extraction, are safer. Both processes begin with unroasted green coffee beans that are soaked in water or steamed so that the caffeine is soluble and ready for extraction. In essence, the caffeine is being worn down so that is can be more easily removed.

Direct extraction is aptly named because the beans come into direct contact with a decaffeinating agent after being softened. An example of this technique is the so-called European process, in which the softened beans are continually rinsed with methylene chloride, a solvent. (Methylene chloride is strictly regulated in both Europe and the United States because it is a carcinogen.) This causes the caffeine to leech out of the beans and form a solution with the methylene chloride. The beans are then removed from the solvent and given another steam to evaporate any re-maining chemicals. Finally, the beans get torched: They're roasted at 450 degrees Fahrenheit, which burns off any solvent residue.

Indirect extraction, on the other hand, occurs when green coffee beans are soaked in a water-based solution called "flavor-charged water." This special water draws out the caffeine as well as a few other oils that are found in coffee. The water is treated with a decaffeinating agent and then is used to impart some flavor back into the decaffeinated beans. After they've been roasted, the beans are good to go.

These methods will recede into history once the naturally caf-feine-free coffee bean takes over the marketplace. Still, the ques-tion will linger: Why would anyone drink decaffeinated coffee in the first place?

Chapter Nine

HEALTH MATTERS

Q Is it true that an apple a day keeps the doctor away?

A It rhymes, so it has to be true! Just like, "No pain, no gain." Oh, wait: That one is patently false since pain can be a very good indication that you're about to seriously injure yourself. Still, the belief in the health benefits of apples dates back to medieval times when the expression was, "Eating an apple before going to bed will make the doctor beg [for] his bread." Let's take a closer look at our good friend the apple and see if it is something more than the perfect pie filling.

The truth is, there is an ever-growing body of research about the preventative and curative powers of the apple, with new maladies being added to the its list of conquests every year. Nutritionists believe that eating apples can help prevent certain types of cancer (including breast, colon, and prostate cancers), reduce bad cholesterol and increase good cholesterol, reduce the risk of strokes or heart attacks, improve lung function and decrease the risk of asthma, and keep your brain sharp while warding off Alzheimer's disease. Pretty remarkable, but we can't help but wonder how one fruit can live up to so many miraculous claims.

The majority of the apple's healing powers are believed to revolve around flavonoids, compounds found in many plants that give them their distinctive colors (i.e., the red in certain apples). In plants, flavonoids act as an immune system of sorts, fighting off pathogens and other harmful elements, such as ultraviolet light.

Flavonoids also can protect the body against the harmful effects of oxidation. Without going too far down the chemistry rabbit hole, if you've ever cut open one of our beloved apples and watched the meat inside turn brown, you've seen oxidation at work—it's a chemical reaction that occurs when oxygen is introduced to a compound. If you're wondering why an apple would turn brown if it's so high in antioxidants, you're not paying attention! We told you that flavonoids give fruits and vegetables their color, so in the case of the apple, they're mostly found in the peel.

Most physicians believe that the antioxidant properties of the apple are what make it so good for you. Of course, there are limits: Antioxidants will not give you immunity to colds or viruses, and no number of apples will save you a trip to the doctor if you, say, accidentally saw off your thumb while building your kid's tree house. Still, eating an apple a day is a sound practice. It will get you a lot further in life than a donut a day.

Q Can stress cause gray hair?

A You can't blame your boss for the fading color of your mane: There is no definitive link between stress and gray hair. What is the reason for that gray in your 'do? A person typically has about one hundred thousand follicles, the sunken, tear-shaped pits in the scalp. The hair-making process takes place at the bottom of each follicle. Keratinocytes (epidermal cells) stack together and produce a strand of hair. Nearby melanocytes manufacture melanin, a pigment delivered to keratinocytes. This pigment determines the color of a person's hair. As a person ages, melanin production slows. As melanin decreases, hair turns gray; if there's no melanin at all, hair is white.

More than anything, genetics seem to determine when hair changes to shades of gray. Silvery strands typically start to emerge for men at around age thirty and for women at thirty-five. In some cases, gray hair can crop up as early as the teen years or as late as the fifties. People of African and Asian ancestry show longer color retention, while 50 percent of Caucasians are 50 percent gray by age fifty. Other factors can affect the process, including environmental influences, vitamin B_{12} deficiencies, and thyroid imbalances.

But what about stress? Since stress affects the resiliency of cells in the body, scientists have hypothesized about its potential relationship to graying hair. Various theories postulate that stress hormones can affect melanocyte survival and activity; cause inflammation at the follicular level, leading to chronic damage and influencing melanin production; or disrupt the delivery signals between melanocytes to keratinocytes.

More research is needed, however, before any of these claims can be termed conclusive. So while you certainly can say that the tyrannical antics of your boss are hair-raising, you can't yet call them hair-graying.

Q Can you grow your own penicillin?

A Mold. Ugh! The slimy stuff covering the leftovers that have been sitting in the fridge for too long. Who needs it? Well, you do if you want to fend off the occasional invasion of deadly bacteria.

Penicillin, one of the world's most powerful antibiotics, is a common form of mold. You've no doubt seen it yourself on bread, potatoes, and other foods. Growing it certainly doesn't take much equipment or skill. Want to try? The British Pharmacological Society recommends the orange method: Pierce a medium-size orange thoroughly with a fork, squeeze it a little to make sure you've gone deep enough to draw out some juice, place it in a shallow dish, and leave it in a cool, dark place at room temperature. After seven to ten days, your orange should sport a fuzzy, bluish-green beard. Penicillin is identified mainly by its color: The blue is *Penicillium italicum;* the green is *Penicillium digitatum.*

Does this mean that applying a piece of moldy fruit to an open wound is a good idea? Could be.

For centuries, folk healers employed mold to fight infections. The remedy didn't always work, however, because penicillin spores are elusive little critters. Under natural conditions, it's difficult to find concentrations dense enough to win a face-off with bacteria.

Antibiotic penicillin is derived from a strain called *Penicillium chrysogenum,* which was first isolated in 1943. During World War II, the search for rich sources of penicillin became desperate. Throughout Allied countries, scientists scoured grocery stores for moldy food. Peoria, Illinois, came up with the winner: a rotten cantaloupe that harbored one of the highest concentrations of penicillin ever seen. This "magic cantaloupe" helped the Allies cook up enough penicillin to save the lives of millions of soldiers. It is no exaggeration to say that penicillin did as much to defeat Germany and Japan as bombs.

How exactly does penicillin work its magic? Bacteria multiply via a process known as binary fission. Penicillin contains a substance called beta-lactam that prevents bacteria from reproducing by inhibiting the formation of cytoplasmic membranes, or new cell walls. If they are unable to successfully divide, the bacteria cannot conquer. Cell walls collapse, and the colony rapidly withers away.

Of course, a few individual bacteria will inevitably prove resistant to penicillin, which is why biochemists are always developing alternative antibiotics. If you have a condition that requires frequent antibiotic use, your doctor will probably try to vary the type just to keep those sneaky bacteria on their toes and out of your corpus. Despite this drawback, penicillin remains one of our mightiest medications, providing generations with longer and healthier lives.

Still wondering what to do with of those slimy leftovers? Throw them out. Please! Like your mom said, cleaning out the fridge is a good way to stay healthy, too.

Q How do vaccines work?

A If you've ever taken a small child to the doctor for a vaccination, you've probably had to explain that a little bit of hurt—a shot, a finger prick, a dose of sour-tasting medicine— can go a long way toward keeping us well. Then that pesky kid invariably asks, "Why?" You shrug and say, "I don't know. It just does, that's all."

Well, here's a better answer to give: superheroes. Your body has its very own superheroes called T cells and B cells. They're both part of your immune system and kick in whenever a virus shows up. Viruses are tiny microbes that can't live outside a body, so once they get inside you, they want to stay and pretty much take over the place. That's when T cells and B cells go to work and kick some butt.

First, "helper" T cells act as scouts, alerting the rest of your immune system to the presence of the invader and relaying the lowdown on its molecular composition. Then "killer" T cells swing into action, destroying any body cells that have been damaged by the virus. Meanwhile, B cells sweep your blood stream to seek out invaders. When they find a viral microbe, the B cells seize it by releasing special antibodies that lock onto the molecules of the virus, slowing it down and making it possible for large white blood cells called macrophages (the foot soldiers of the immune system) to come and eliminate it. Only one type of antibody will capture any given virus. Once the virus has been defeated, your immune system will remember which antibody it used and will be prepared should that particular unwelcome guest show up again.

What does all of this have to do with vaccines? When you are vaccinated, a doctor injects a tiny bit of a disease into your body. This may consist of a few very weak microbes or an artificial duplicate that researchers produce in a lab. Your body reacts as if the virus was the real thing—it's kind of like having an immune system fire drill. Your B cells manufacture the correct antibodies and add them to your arsenal of immune defenses. In short, you now have superpowers against some dangerous diseases. Pretty cool, huh?

Why don't vaccines work against every disease? Because not all illnesses are brought on by viruses. Some are caused by bacteria and cured by antibiotics. Some are the result of poor nutrition. Others have no known cure. The vaccinations we do have, however, make the world a much healthier place. They have helped many of us live long and prosper. And it doesn't get much more super than that.

Q Does chocolate really cause pimples?

A Hey, are you still reading dermatology books from the 1950s? Since then, tons of research has revealed that

Snickers, Whatchamacallit, and Mr. Goodbar are not responsible for the outbreak of carbuncles on your face. Need proof?

Back in 1969, doctors at the University of Pennsylvania School of Medicine took sixty-five pizza-faced adolescents and gave them either bittersweet chocolate bars (which contained ten times the amount of chocolate that is found in your typical candy bar) or identical-looking bars that contained no real chocolate. After one month, those who ate the excessive amounts of real chocolate every day (lucky ducks) showed no signs of increased or worsened acne.

A later study, which was conducted with eighty acne-afflicted midshipmen at the U.S. Naval Academy in Annapolis, showed similar results. Eating chocolate does not seem to give rise to whiteheads, blackheads, papules, or pustules. And subsequent research has continued to demonstrate that acne is not primarily linked to diet. In fact, no one food has ever been proven to cause acne. This means that you can eat anything and everything without worrying about developing a nasty case of acne, pizza and potato chips included!

What does cause acne? Science has not been able to pinpoint an exact source. That's because there are several complicated factors—including hormones, environment, and heredity (thanks, Mom and Dad)—at play.

On a basic level, we know that pimples pop up when skin pores get clogged, either with dead skin cells and excess oil or with greasy ingredients from applied cosmetics, moisturizers, and such. Technically, chocolate could cause a pimple or two—but only if you melted a bunch of it and rubbed it all over your face.

Q Does eating after *8:00* PM cause you to gain weight?

A It seems logical enough: You eat a huge cheesesteak, hit the hay a few hours later, and lay there like a lump, burning off only negligible calories when you roll over or unconsciously pass wind. Naturally, one would expect all of those calories to turn into fat by sunrise. But medical degrees aren't handed out to people who buy into a theory because it seems logical. Scientists with actual credentials have looked into this issue— specifically, in a study at Oregon Health and Science University in 2006—and proved once again that logic doesn't always equal medical fact.

To conduct their study, researchers fed a group of rhesus monkeys (whose DNA is a 93 percent match to that of humans) identical high-fat diets. They monitored the times that the monkeys ate and found a wide range of results. Some monkeys ate more than half of their daily calories at night, while others consumed as little as 6 percent after dark—the monkeys' eating habits were essentially in step with those of people. The monkeys all had the same weight gain, no matter when they ate. The study concluded that the timing of food intake isn't a factor in weight gain.

The issue, however, doesn't end there. Some doctors suggest that the habit of eating at night is linked to poor dietary choices that can result in weight gain. For example, some people might be too busy to eat before 8:00 PM and end up hitting a fast-food drive-through at night. Or they might wait so long to have dinner that they become ravenous and eat enormous portions to compensate. Or at the end of a long day, they lose the will to stick to a strict diet and eat whatever they want.

The bottom line: Eat as late at night as you want—just don't stay at the table too long.

Q Does putting raw meat on a black eye really help?

A We've long believed that everything you need to know in life can be learned from Saturday morning cartoons. Popeye teaches us that spinach makes you strong, Elmer Fudd shows us that it's fun to laugh at people with speech impediments, and Scooby Doo proves to us that meddling kids make the best detectives. And from Fred Flintstone we get this gem of a remedy: Nothing treats a black eye like applying a slab of meat to it.

Unfortunately, it turns out that obtaining medical advice from Saturday morning cartoons probably isn't a great idea. Despite the wonders that raw meat works for Fred and Barney, doctors agree that applying a T-bone to a black eye isn't going to help much.

In fact, putting raw meat anywhere near your eye probably isn't the best idea. Uncooked meat is not only laden with bacteria, but it's also a prime carrier of *E. coli,* a really gnarly bacterium that often causes bloody diarrhea and potential kidney failure. If you really feel the need to press meat against your eye, make sure it's wrapped and frozen. Applying an ice pack (in this case, one that is composed of meat) can help reduce swelling.

The next time you have a medical emergency, it might be wiser to visit a doctor than to consult Fred Flintstone. Just make sure that the doc's instruments aren't made by the Acme Corporation.

Q Does sticking needles into the body really cure what ails you?

A What we're talking about here is the ancient art of acupuncture. Practitioners of acupuncture believe that stimulation of specific points on the body eases the flow of an energy called *qi* (pronounced "chee"), which helps to restore the body's natural balance of yin and yang.

Yeah, we know what you're thinking: "Give me a break. What's next? Using The Force?" Though acupuncture does have a fairly high snicker factor, you should keep in mind that it has been practiced for thousands of years and has a legion of faithful supporters who swear that it can work miracles. Let's take a closer look at the facts.

Acupuncture is a staple of Traditional Chinese medicine (TCM)— and when we say "traditional," we mean "really old." The first written account of acupuncture dates back to around 200 BC. As we said, a fundamental principle of TCM is the idea that the body is in a sensitive state of balance between the forces of yin and yang. When your yin and yang are out of whack, your *qi* cannot flow correctly through your body along its natural pathways, called meridians. According to the tenets of TCM, disease and other health problems stem from an imbalance of these two forces; methods like acupuncture are used to put the body back into equilibrium. Essentially, you stick needles into the meridians to increase the flow of *qi*, and you feel like a million bucks.

Acupuncture became popular in the United States after a 1971 article in the *New York Times* praised its ability to relieve pain. A 2002 study by the National Institutes of Health (NIH) estimated that more than eight million Americans have turned to acupuncture at some point in their lives. Acupuncture has even been embraced by Western medicine to a slight degree, as both the NIH and the U.S. Food and Drug Administration have endorsed acupuncture as a safe—and possibly effective—medical option.

Does it work? If you're looking for hard evidence regarding the existence of *qi,* give it up. You'd have an easier time proving the existence of UFOs. *Qi* could be a metaphor for the electrical signals that run along the body through the nervous system or—like many of the notions about medicine that are thousands of years old—a complete load. Researchers have been unable to prove that acupuncture is effective for treating a number of conditions, although it does seem to be able to raise a person's tolerance for pain, thus making it a semi-acceptable treatment for pain relief. Jab enough needles into your body and you'll get used to the uncomfortable sensation, right?

But that's about as far as we can go down the New Age trail. Sticking needles into your body probably isn't going to cure what ails you—unless the needles are delivering medicine or you're trying to pop a blister.

Q Does popping a zit make it go away faster?

A Yes, but only if you pop the right kind of zit and do it the right way. What's the right kind of zit? Look for a ripe, juicy white one that appears to be on the verge of a major eruption. Any deep, painful cysts or nodules (you know, the ones with their own pulse), should be left alone or injected with a shot of inflammation-reducing cortisone by your friendly neighborhood dermatologist.

Other pimples to avoid include those above nose-level on your face. Why? The veins around your forehead drain directly into the brain, so squeezing down on zits in this area can actually push bacteria into your gray matter—and you'll end up with much bigger problems than a slightly embarrassing blemish.

Now that that's settled, let's move on to the popping. This is kind of Minor Surgery 101, so please pay attention. First of all, the best time to pop a zit is right after a hot, steamy shower, when your skin is clean and supple and zits have risen to the surface. You might be tempted to just go at 'em with your fingers, but that will only create more redness, swelling, and maybe Freddy Krueger-esque scarring.

The right way to pop a zit—at least according to dermatologist Jeffrey Benabio, who has written scientific articles on this kind of thing—is with a needle (a sharp sewing needle is best). The first thing you must do is sterilize it. Next, take the sterilized needle and hold it parallel to your skin. You're going to lance the pimple at the top of one end and slide the needle through to the other end. Don't worry, this won't hurt a bit—the skin covering the pimple is already dead.

Once the needle is through, gently pull up to open the skin. If the pimple is ripe for the picking, the pus will begin to drain out freely. Finally, clean what's left of the zit with an alcohol-soaked cotton ball or a little witch hazel.

As for those who say you should never pick a pimple, they've probably never had one big enough to inspire total mortification. Truth is, self-grooming is a common practice among all primate animals, not just humans. If you pop your pimples appropriately, they can be off your face—and out of your life—in about seventy-two hours.

Chapter Ten

HISTORY

Q Are human beings still evolving?

A Before tackling this one, we need to give you a quick history of human evolution. The creatures that became *homo sapiens* (humans) split from apes between two and four million years ago. A common theory is that everyone started in Africa and slowly spread out across the world. Once isolated from each other, we all evolved slightly differently, which accounts for qualities like different skin colors.

Nowadays, however, we're no longer geographically isolated, so we're unlikely to evolve into an entirely new species. But evolution doesn't just refer to the development of a new species—it's tricky to define. Some people see evolution as a change over time in the gene pool—that's all the genes from all living humans. If that's the case, we *are* still evolving. Each generation has random mutations that may get passed on. These aren't just noticeable changes like albinism or blindness, but also alterations like someone growing up to be a bit taller than usual. Some people have more offspring than others, so more of their genes get passed on, and the gene pool shifts as a result.

Many people prefer to think of evolution as a slow change to the gene pool that is caused by natural selection. Natural selection is a theory that was developed by Charles Darwin: Some random mutations give certain individuals an advantage, and these people survive long enough to have offspring. Maybe the slightly taller person can reach the healthier fruit on the taller trees, for instance. Scientists argue, but the consensus is that we are still evolving according to this theory.

Recent studies have shown that we've evolved in several ways relatively recently. Researchers at the University of Chicago found two new genes that are involved in developing the brain. One is a version of microcephalin that emerged about 37,000 years ago and is now carried by 70 percent of the global population. The other is a variant of something called the ASPM (abnormal spindle-like microcephaly-associated, if you must know) gene, which arose 5,800 years ago and is now present in about 30 percent of humans.

These two genes coincide with the introduction of new ways of living. The microcephalin gene arrived on the scene in the same period as art, music, sophisticated stone tools, and religious practices. The ASPM variant arose at about the time humans began shifting from hunting and gathering to agriculture and large settlements.

Some people argue that certain races are more evolved than others. But the reality is that everyone has been evolving pretty equally, just in different ways. For instance, Europeans have been found to be more likely to break down lactose (a sugar that is found in milk, which they would have had plenty of from all those cows and goats) than other cultures. On the other hand, several tribes in Northern Africa can break down mannose (a sweet substance found in some plants) more easily, because they've been eating it longer.

So yes, we're evolving, but don't ask scientists what we're evolving into. Evolution is an unpredictable.

Q Did Betsy Ross really make the first American flag?

A American history is big business. Each year tourists flock to historical sites, where they spend millions of dollars on replicas of the Declaration of Independence, ceramic busts of George Washington, lunches at fake colonial taverns, and Liberty

Bell snow globes. Not that we're complaining—we love historical snow globes as much as the next patriot. But this massive tourist economy depends less on actual history and more on good stories (or myths, as some sticklers might call them).

Some of these stories are widely recognized as myths: George Washington chopping down the cherry tree, for example. But the origins of others are murkier. For example: Did Betsy Ross sew the first American flag?

For those of you who have forgotten your grade-school pageants, the Betsy Ross tale goes something like this: In May 1776, three members of the Continental Congress, including Washington himself, visited humble seamstress Betsy Ross with a secret request: They needed a flag for the soon-to-be United States of America. Betsy, who was an expert seamstress as well as a remarkable woman (she lost two husbands to the Revolution), immediately set to work creating the enduring symbol of freedom and glory. It's a great story, told and re-told in history pageants from sea to shining sea. The only problem is, it's probably not true.

Considering how thoroughly much of the struggle for independence is documented, there is surprisingly little in the historical record about the origin of the Stars and Stripes, possibly because contemporary chroniclers were more concerned with a little thing called the Revolution. In fact, nobody cared much about who sewed the first American flag until March 1870, when historian William Canby presented a paper to the Philadelphia Historical Society that proclaimed Betsy Ross as the mother of the American flag. Betsy Ross was Canby's grandmother, and his historical evidence was primarily the affidavits of his relatives and the memories of a few ancient people who were nearing senility. In absence of other definitive evidence, the public quickly latched onto Canby's claim and elevated Betsy Ross from simple seamstress to Mother of Freedom.

Nowadays, few legitimate historians support the tale, pointing out, among other things, that George Washington was probably more concerned with patching together his army than with visiting humble seamstresses to talk flag design. Historians also point out that Francis Hopkinson, a signer of the Declaration of Independence, submitted a bill to Congress requesting compensation for his design of the American flag; this is the only documented evidence of anyone claiming responsibility. Indeed, most historians—and the United States government—recognize Hopkinson as the original designer.

Still, Betsy's legend is powerful. Perhaps it's no surprise that in surveys polling American students, Betsy Ross is among the most famous non-presidential Americans in history.

Q Why does everyone clap so much during the State of the Union address?

Earlier tonight, it was George Bush's State of the Union address... He was interrupted forty times by applause and twice to look up a word in the dictionary.
—David Letterman

A The Constitution requires only that the President "shall from time to time give to Congress information of the State of the

Union and recommend to their consideration such measures as he shall judge necessary and expedient." There's nothing in there mandating massive applause, but it's a signature of the occasion just the same.

The State of the Union was meant to be like the British monarch's Speech from the Throne, given at the opening of Parliament each year. George Washington gave the first State of the Union speech in January 1790. Third president Thomas Jefferson thought the practice was too British and instead sent a written statement to be read by a clerk; this was the standard until Woodrow Wilson delivered the message to Congress in 1913. Calvin Coolidge's 1923 speech was the first to be broadcast on the radio; Harry Truman's in 1947 the first to be shown on television; and George W. Bush's in 2002 the first to be Webcast on the Internet.

But what about the applause? The State of the Union address takes place in the U.S. Capitol Building, and begins when the Sergeant at Arms of the U.S. House of Representatives calls out, "Mister/Madam Speaker, the President of the United States!" The doors of the House Chamber are opened, and a standing ovation is expected. The members of Congress are not applauding the person—note that the Sergeant at Arms does not refer to the president by name—but rather the office of President. The hardy bipartisan welcome is a show of patriotism.

Once the audience is settled, the Speaker of the House raps the gavel and again introduces the president—but not by name. Again, the applause is for the office. When the president begins to speak, he is interrupted by applause many times, some of which becomes partisan in nature. During George W. Bush's fifty-three-minute State of the Union speech in 2008, he was interrupted seventy-two times by applause, often only by Republicans. However, mentions of greenhouse gases and job retraining prompted Democrats to jump to their feet because these are Democratic party issues.

One member of Congress is notably absent from the State of the Union address because of the theoretical possibility that the country would be left without a leader if the Capitol Building were attacked and everyone were wiped out. This person is called the President pro Tempore of the Senate. In 2008, it was West Virginia Senator Robert Byrd, who watched the speech from the comfort of his own home. No word on whether Byrd applauded.

Q Was there really a guy named Johnny Appleseed?

A Someone named Johnny Appleseed traipsing around in bare feet, with a tin kettle on his head. No, we're not describing the latest nut-job on a Fox reality series. Believe it or not, there really was a man who went by the moniker Johnny Appleseed. While some of the stories about him are suspect—especially the bit about the tin kettle on his head—he is an important part of the history of the United States.

He was born John Chapman in 1774 in Leominster, Massachusetts; his father was a Minuteman who fought for the Continental Army during the Revolutionary War. Little is known about Johnny's daily life when he growing up or when he was a young man. At about the age of twenty-six, he headed to the developing Midwest. In Pennsylvania, he picked up a load of apple seeds from cider presses and moved into what would become Ohio. There, he planted apple nurseries along streams, rivers, and creeks. Before long, his fellow pioneers started calling him Johnny Appleseed.

He was not a seed scatterer, as some people think, but rather one of the founding fathers of the nursery industry. Johnny tended to his apple nurseries and started new ones whenever he found a good spot. He didn't plant all of his seedlings for free: While he would give some away to new settlers and Native Americans, he often charged six cents for a seedling. He also accepted cornmeal or old clothes as barter if people didn't have money.

Johnny lived simply. He really did go around without shoes, slept outdoors, and most likely wore castoff clothing. But he was not poor. He donated the money he earned from his nurseries to charity or used it to further his business. Chapman spent nearly fifty years planting nursery after nursery in what is now Pennsylvania, Ohio, Indiana, Illinois, and Kentucky. Some of his trees still bear fruit.

Why apples? Johnny believed that apples would be important to the development of the Midwest, which then was mostly wilderness. Apple trees were easy to grow, and the fruit was versatile: Apples could be made into butter and cider, and could be dried and saved for use during the winter months.

Johnny's deeds made him revered along the frontier by settlers and Native Americans alike. The next time you're in a Midwest state and are about to bite into an apple, take a moment to reflect on the significance of the tasty fruit—just don't commemorate the occasion by putting a tin kettle on your head.

Q Can a war hero's statue tell you whether he died in battle?

A It depends on where you are. In one particular national park, yes; everywhere else, no.

An urban legend that lots of tour guides and park rangers have kept alive is that if the hero is on a horse, you can tell how he fared in battle. Here's how it's supposed to work: If the horse has all four feet on the ground, the rider survived the fight intact. One leg lifted—the rider was wounded. Two legs lifted—the rider died in battle.

This is true if you're at Gettysburg National Military Park in Pennsylvania, which is filled with statues of men on horseback. For example, Union General George Meade's mount has all its feet touching the metal base of his statue, while General Winfield S. Hancock's horse has a leg raised. Meade came through the three-day Battle of Gettysburg without a scratch, but Hancock was wounded (a bullet struck his saddle, then both the bullet and a saddle nail pierced his thigh). The one exception to the rule at Gettysburg is a memorial to General James Longstreet, which was erected in 1998. The horse has a leg lifted, but Longstreet was not injured at that battlefield.

In places other than Gettysburg, the rule doesn't hold up as well. General Stonewall Jackson's horse at Manassas National Battle-field Park in Virginia has four feet on the ground, but Jackson was killed by "friendly fire" during the Civil War. Outside the White House, a statue of another Jackson, President Andrew Jackson, shows the horse on two legs, but Jackson died of tuberculosis at age seventy-eight, not in battle.

In fact, if you tally all the equestrian statues with riders in Washington, D.C., only a third conform to the alleged rule—exactly the result that a random distribution would suggest. There are only three possible positions for a standing horse statue, after all: four feet on the ground, or three, or two. (No horse statue could balance on one leg.)

So if there are indeed rules for statues of war heroes, someone forgot to tell most of the sculptors.

Q Couldn't the Irish have found something to eat besides potatoes to avoid a famine?

A More than a million people starved to death in Ireland from 1845 to 1851. The disaster is called the Great Famine, but it wasn't really a famine. Only one crop failed: the potato. How could this have killed so many? Why didn't the Irish eat cabbage or scones or even chalupas, for crying out loud?

The answer is simple: Those who starved were poor. For generations, the impoverished in Ireland had survived by planting potatoes to feed their families. They had nothing else. Ireland's wealthy landowners grew a wide variety of crops, but these were shipped away and sold for profit. Most of the rich folks didn't care that the poor starved.

How did things get so bad? Irish History 101: The Catholics and the Protestants didn't like each other, and neither did the English and the Irish. Back then, the wealthy landowners were mostly Protestants from England, while the poor were Catholic peasants.

The Irish peasants grew their food on small parcels of land that were rented from the hated English.

In the sixteenth century, a hitherto unknown item crossed the Atlantic from Peru, originally arriving in England and finally getting to Ireland in 1590: the potato. Spuds grew well in Ireland, even on the rocky, uneven plots that were often rented by peasants, and they quickly became the peasants' main food source. Potatoes required little labor to grow, and an acre could yield twelve tons of them—enough to feed a family of six for the entire year, with leftovers for the animals.

We think of potatoes as a fattening food, but they're loaded with vitamins, carbohydrates, and even some protein. Add a little fish and buttermilk to the diet, and a family could live quite happily on potatoes. Potatoes for breakfast, lunch, and dinner might sound monotonous, but it fueled a population boom in Ireland. By the nineteenth century, three million people were living on the potato diet.

In 1845, though, the fungus *Phytophthora infestans,* or "late blight," turned Ireland's potatoes into black, smelly, inedible lumps. Impoverished families had no options, no Plan B. Their pitiful savings were wiped out, and they fled to the work houses—the only places where they could get food and shelter in return for their labor.

When the potato crop failed again the next year, and every year through 1849, people began dying in earnest—not just from starvation, but from scurvy and gangrene (caused by a lack of vitamin C), typhus, dysentery, typhoid fever, and heart failure. Overwhelmed and underfunded, the work houses closed their doors.

Many people who were weakened by hunger died of exposure after being evicted from their homes. To top the disaster off, a cholera epidemic spread during the last year of the blight, killing thousands more.

The exact number of those who perished is unknown, but it's believed to be between one and two million. In addition, at least a million people left the country, and many of these wayward souls died at sea. All during that terrible time, plenty of food existed in Ireland, but it was consumed by the wealthy. The poor, meanwhile, had nothing. They were left to starve.

Q Did princesses ever wear glass slippers?

A Every little girl dreams of having a fairy godmother who, with the wave of a magic wand, turns her pajamas into a beautiful gown and her stuffed animals into a coterie of courtiers to escort her to a royal ball where a valiant prince will choose her for his princess. We apologize to any little girls who are reading this, but we've got some bad news: Life is not a fairy tale. You're not going to turn a pumpkin into a carriage, and you're certainly not going to be wearing any glass slippers. Sorry. That's just the way it is.

Princesses never wore glass slippers. But to learn how this most famous detail of the Cinderella story came to be, we need to go back to the time of seventeenth-century writer Charles Perrault, one of the first Europeans to record fairy tales that had been orally passed from generation to generation for hundreds of years.

The Cinderella tale—in which a poor girl who is tormented by her stepfamily wins the love of a prince with the help of her fairy godmother—is one of the oldest and most widespread stories in world folklore. Versions of the tale date as far back as at least AD 850. For most of history, a glass slipper played no part in the story. In many of the tales, the slipper was made of fur, though in some versions shoes and slippers were made of silk, satin, or precious metals. There was another, somewhat gory plot point many of these stories shared: The cruel stepsisters mutilated their feet attempting to fit into the magic shoe.

Perrault first brought the glass slipper into the fairy-tale lexicon. How this came about is a matter of debate among historians. Some argue that Perrault, who was working from oral tradition, simply misunderstood what he heard—the word *vair* (French for "fur") sounds much like the word *verre* (French for "glass"). Others hold that English translators made the mistake when transcribing Perrault's French version.

Either way, when Perrault published his seminal *Histoires ou Contes du Temps Passé* in 1697, the glass slipper appeared on Cinderella's foot. The book spawned an entire Cinderella industry, which banks on hope. Foolish, foolish hope.

Q Did Troy exist?

A Sure. Troy Aikman, Troy Donahue, Troy, Michigan—which one do you want to read about? Oh, you're thinking about Troy, the site of the Trojan War? Yup, that existed too.

If you remember your history classes—or if you saw the movie—you know that Troy was the walled city of the Trojans. Troy's Prince Paris stole the beautiful Helen from her husband in Sparta and carried her back to Troy. The disgruntled husband and all his kingly friends began a war that lasted ten years and ended with Troy's destruction. This was chronicled in *The Iliad,* Europe's oldest epic poem. How old? Perhaps three thousand years old.

The Greeks and Romans never doubted that Troy had been a real place, situated near the Dardanelles—today, a part of Turkey. In 1870, a German-born archaeologist named Heinrich Schliemann announced that he'd discovered the ruins of Troy. Schliemann dug into a mound called Hisarlik and found layers of ancient cities, each built on the ruins of earlier settlements. He found (or possibly faked) gold treasures, but it was his assistant—Wilhelm Dörpfeld—who later realized that no fewer than nine separate cities had been built on that spot. Conveniently, they're labeled Troy I through Troy IX.

Troy I began as a Stone Age village around 3600 BC. Over the millennia, it evolved into a royal city. Schliemann assumed that remains near the bottom of his excavation—Troy II—were from the real Troy, because Troy II was destroyed by fire. *That* fortified city, though, dates back to 2300 BC—far too early to be the Troy of legend. Scholars today believe that *The Iliad's* Troy is probably Troy VIIa, built on the ruins of a richer city that was destroyed by an earthquake in the twelfth century BC.

How much of *The Iliad* is based on fact? We will probably never know, partly because very little evidence can survive for three thousand years, but mostly because Schliemann's excavation methods destroyed more than they saved.

From 1982 until his death in 2005, German archaeologist Manfred Korfmann made more discoveries near the site of Troy. He found that a fifty-foot-high burial mound, long called the Tomb of Achilles, did indeed date from the time of Troy VIIa. Korfmann also excavated a cemetery with more than fifty Greek graves from the same period. Swords and pottery imply that Greek aristocrats were buried there, along with women and children. What's more, Korfmann may have found the ancient harbor and camp where most of *The Iliad*'s action took place. Although not every scholar and archaeologist accepts this site as ancient Troy, it was declared a UNESCO World Heritage Site in 1998.

Now, about Troy Aikman...

Q How are old coins taken out of circulation?

A To answer this question, let's track some money from beginning to end. What follows is the tale of Dimey (a dime) and Bill (a dollar bill).

Dimey is one of the nearly fifteen billion coins that was minted at the United States Mints in Philadelphia and Denver in 2007, and Bill is one of the thirty-eight million notes printed in one day during the same year at the Bureau of Engraving and Printing in Washington, D.C., and Fort Worth, Texas.

Off they go to Federal Reserve Banks around the country, excited to be part of $820 billion in circulation. Their journey isn't finished when they get to the Federal Reserve Banks, though. They still have to go to a couple of commercial banks. There they sit and wait, talking about life, the universe, and the latest episode of *American Idol*—until one day someone withdraws them to pay for a new shirt at a dodgy roadside stall. The owner of the stall then spends Dimey on some candy and uses Bill and some of his dollar friends to get into a baseball game. Thus begins a long, adventure-filled journey for both Dimey and Bill. They meet all sorts of people and grow old and worn.

About twenty-one months later—the normal lifespan for a dollar note—Bill winds up in a bank again. The bank manager takes one look at him and dumps him onto the "unfit" pile. After a while, he is packed up and sent to a Reserve Bank. There, he is cruelly replaced with a younger, hipper dollar bill and is destroyed. (About a third of the money that the Reserve Banks receive is declared unfit and is destroyed.)

Tragic, right? It gets worse.

Meanwhile, Dimey is making the rounds. He meets a cute commemorative-dollar coin down someone's sofa, and they have a brief affair before the dollar is dropped into a jar for safekeeping. Dimey is once again sent of his way. About twenty-five years later, Dimey is old and worn, but he still fits into all the machine slots, so he thinks he's just as good as any of the young whippersnap-per dimes.

But one day, he ends up at the same bank where Bill was unceremoniously heaved onto the "unfit" pile years

OLD

earlier. And the same mean bank manager is still in charge. The manager doesn't like the look of Dimey, either, and sends him to a Reserve Bank. From there, he is put into a box with other worn coins. Next to them is a box that is filled with badly damaged coins.

Off they all go back to the Mint, where they see their shiny new replacements heading off to the banks. Then Dimey and his fellow old coins are tipped into a furnace and melted down.

But it's not all doom and gloom for Dimey and company. In the coin equivalent of reincarnation, they're recycled and become parts of new dimes.

Q Do all countries have military forces?

A Who wants to know? You looking to start some trouble? Okay, we give: There are twenty-one countries that do not have formal forces. Some have components of a military, such as a Coast Guard, while others have relatively large police forces that may dabble in a little national security on the side.

Most countries that do not have sustainable defensive military forces have a "you scratch my back, and I'll get my back scratched" deal with other nations. France, for instance, is responsible for Monaco, and it shares the responsibility of defending Andorra with Spain. Australia and New Zealand would help out Kiribati if needed. New Zealand must consider all requests for military aid by Samoa in accordance with the most sweetly named treaty ever, the Treaty of Friendship (1962). And of course, Italy would probably have something to say to anyone who tried to mess with the Rome-based Vatican City, although Italy and the Vatican do not have a defense treaty because it would violate the Vatican's neutrality.

Beginning in 1951, Iceland had a deal with the United States that had U.S. military forces stationed there until 2006, when they withdrew. While the United States no longer has a physical presence there, Iceland and the United States have signed a Joint Understanding to continue a "bilateral defense relationship." Since Iceland does have a Coast Guard, there are some things Iceland can share with us. In addition to Iceland, the United States is responsible for defending the Marshall Islands, the Federated States of Micronesia, and Palau, since they are official associated states—free entities with political ties to the United States.

Dominica, Grenada, Saint Lucia, and Saint Vincent and the Grenadines do not have official military forces, but they are all protected under the Regional Security System (RSS). The RSS is an agreement among many Caribbean countries to protect one another.

Haiti, Costa Rica, and a few other small countries don't have militaries, but they do have extensive police forces, some of which have paramilitary units. Haiti's military, while disbanded, still exists on paper in its Constitution.

So, while some countries aren't exactly armed to the teeth, it would still require more than a few drunken friends and some slingshots to take them over.

Q How many human languages are there?

A *Moi! Natya! Malo! O-si-yo!* That's hello in Finnish, Kikuyu, Samoan, and Cherokee, respectively. How many different languages are there? By one count: 6,912. That's a lot of hellos. It's also a lot of good-byes: Nearly five hundred of these languages have fewer than one hundred fluent speakers and are in danger of dying out within a generation.

By contrast, Mandarin Chinese is spoken by about 1.05 billion people. This includes both the 882 million native speakers and 178 million who speak it as a second language, adding up to nearly a sixth of the world's population. Hindi/Urdu or Hindustani, the primary language of the subcontinent of India, is spoken natively by 451 million people and by another 453 million as a second language. English comes in third with 337 million native speakers, plus 350 million who use it as a second language.

At the bottom of the list are Comanche, a Native American language with only two hundred fluent speakers; Livonian, a Latvian language spoken by thirty-five people; and a combination of Sami dialects from the reindeer herding tribes of northern Scandinavia with fewer than forty speakers each.

Who's counting languages, and why? For many years, the *Ethnologue* has been the most reliable source of information on world languages. This organization, started by Christian missionaries who were interested in translating the Bible into every known language, partnered with the International Organization for Standardization in 2002 to create a coding system for tracking languages. Recently, the *Observatoire de Linguistique,* a European research network, and *Encarta,* the encyclopedia published by Microsoft, have also released their own language indices.

Not all of these sources agree. There may be as few as five thousand languages or as many as eleven thousand, depending on which method linguists use to distinguish dialects from full-fledged languages. They all reach the same conclusion, however: As the globe's population increases, the number of unique languages decreases. Every language, no matter how obscure, represents part of humanity's cultural inheritance. Some researchers have concluded that half the world's current languages will die out by the end of the twenty-first century, taking much of their history, music, and literature with them.

Fortunately, the future of linguistic diversity may not be that dire. Languages can demonstrate surprising resiliency. Witness the persistence of Yiddish. Not so dead yet, *nu?* However, Walmajarri (Australia, one thousand speakers), Inuinnaqtun (Canada, two thousand speakers), and Culina (Peru/Brazil, 1,300 speakers) may not be so lucky.

Maybe we should all brush up on our language skills before it's too late. Get a bilingual dictionary, take a deep breath, and learn how to say, "Hello."

Q What are ziggurats?

A Everybody's heard of the pyramids of Egypt, but what about the ziggurats of Mesopotamia? Starting in the fourth millennium BC, more than two thousand years before the Egyptians built the Great Pyramid of Cheops, the Sumerians in Mesopotamia were busy constructing mighty towers in an attempt to reach all the way up to heaven. Or at least that's what the Bible tells us.

The word *ziggurat* comes from Akkadian, one of the earliest languages of the Near East. It means "to build on a raised area." Ziggurats resembled huge wedding cakes made of brick and clay. The tallest towers consisted of seven layers.

How high were these ziggurats? Not very, according to our standards. The temple of Borsippa, one of the largest ziggurats that has been excavated by archaeologists, is estimated to have stood 231 feet—or approximately seventy meters—high at completion. That's only a little less than a fifth as tall as the Empire State Building (1,250 feet) and less than one-fourth the height of the Eiffel Tower (984 feet). But on the relatively flat terrain of the Tigris-Euphrates valley, it's easy to see how that height would have impressed the locals.

Joseph Campbell, a famous scholar of world mythology, believed the ziggurats were regarded by the Sumerians as connectors between the earth and heaven. The lowest layers represented the original mound from which the earth was created, and the top layer served as a temple where the gods could dwell and look out over the land.

Did the Tower of Babel, a type of ziggurat, actually exist? About fifty to sixty miles south of contemporary Baghdad lie the remains of what archaeologists think is the ancient city of Babylon. There, they have uncovered the first layer of a temple whose name is

Etemenanki, according to cuneiform tablets, which translates to "the foundation between heaven and earth." This temple must have been important because it was reconstructed several times over the centuries, most notably by King Nebuchadnezzar II around 600 BC.

King Neb, as you may recall, is one of the great villains of the Bible. Dubbed the "Destroyer of Nations" by the prophet Jeremiah, he conquered Jerusalem in 587 BC, demolishing King Solomon's Temple and dragging the Hebrews off into slavery and exile in Babylon. After witnessing the destruction of their own house of worship, the Hebrews had ample reason to resent Babylon and its seven-story ziggurat.

Babylon itself fell to Alexander the Great in 331 BC. After that, any attempt to repair *Etemenanki* always seemed to end in disaster, and it eventually crumbled into a single, low mound. The story, however, lives on, and with it our fascination with the ancient people whose towers once tried to join the earth with the sky.

Chapter Eleven

EARTH AND SPACE

Q Do trees have sex?

A Birds do it. Bees do it. Even your friendly neighborhood trees do it. Does that mean the maples, elms, and oaks are getting it on in the park after dark? No. Only a minority of trees exhibit what biologists would term sexual dimorphism, meaning that each member of a species is either male or female and displays characteristics distinct to that gender. Trees with two separate sexes are dioecious.

So if you're still waiting for that holly you planted last Christmas to bear berries, you might be in for a disappointment. He's probably pining for a mate: The female holly produces the berries.

And these gals are not into long-distance relationships. In order to reproduce, two holly trees must be no more than one hundred yards apart—pretty close for a pair of trees. Not that there's any commingling of roots and leaves: Bees do the work, transporting pollen from the male to the female.

Sounds pretty basic. Just like what you learned in Biology 101. But then things among trees start to get a little wild. About 5 to 7 percent of all species of trees are dioecious, including the juniper, cedar, and ash. A roughly equal percentage are monoecious. Monoecious trees—such as the black walnut, dogwood, and magnolia—have both male and female flowers on the same plant. The remaining 85 to 90 percent of trees are hermaphrodites. Yes, that's the botanical term. Each flower contains both male and female parts—stamen with pollen for the male and pistils with ovaries and eggs for the female. These hermaphrodite blossoms are known as angiosperms, or "perfect" flowers.

The sexual variations don't stop there. Some female dioecious trees also have hermaphrodite flowers, making them gynodioecious. Calimyrna fig trees, which are famous for their delicious fruit, tend to be this way. Male trees with hermaphrodite flowers are androdioecious. Some monoecious trees switch back and forth, bearing flowers of one sex one year and the other sex the next. Those that start out female and transition to male are protogynous; the ones that do the reverse are protoandrous. Dioecious trees that perform this switch trick are polygamo-dioecious. They can be either male or female, but not both at once. Is your head spinning yet? Consider this: A few trees, like the carob, mix it all up, bearing male, female, and hermaphrodite flowers at the same time. These trees are trioecious.

Of course, trees don't like to pollinate themselves, even when they can. (It's bad for the spe-cies.) To swap pollen with one another, they have to draw all kinds of other creatures into the act, including insects, birds, small mammals, and even people. Wind and water are other key components. When you brush by a flowering tree or lean over to smell a blossom, you might be doing more than simply enjoying na-ture—you might be joining in a tree's idea of a threesome.

Come to think of it, the oaks, elms, maples, hollies, hickories, pines, and poplars *are* getting it on in the park. Even when it's not dark.

Q Why doesn't water in a water tower freeze?

A Although our chemistry teacher more likely compared us to Linus Van Pelt than Linus Pauling, even we know that water freezes at thirty-two degrees Fahrenheit. Which is why we've never been able to understand why water doesn't freeze in water towers during those long, cold winters.

To fully understand why you're able to turn on your faucet and have running water even on the coldest days, we need to look at how water towers work. Most towns get their water from wells or bodies of water such as lakes. This water is pumped to a water treatment plant, where it is disinfected before being delivered through a main pipeline to the rest of the area's delivery system.

A water tower is hooked up to that system, drawing water into its reservoir as it is pumped through the main pipes. When the demand for water is too much for the system pump to handle, gravity and water pressure release water from the tower back into the main pipeline. During off-peak times, the water tower refills from the pipeline.

This is a simple, efficient system, and one that helps explain why water towers don't freeze solid in the winter. When a water tower pulls water from the pipeline to refill its reservoir, it is drawing somewhat warmer water from the pipes. Furthermore, water towers are drained and refilled fairly frequently, making it difficult for ice to form. The agitation of water molecules from the movement of draining and refilling slows down the freezing process, too. (To get an idea of the way this works, think of how long it takes waterfalls or rivers to freeze.)

However, in some parts of the country—such as the frozen tundra of North Dakota—water in water towers does freeze. Rarely, though, does it freeze solid. In climates where freezing is a danger, water towers are more heavily insulated, and some are even built with heating systems near their bases that prevent water from freezing on its way into the tower.

Of course, no precautions are foolproof. Just about anything can freeze over if it's cold enough for long enough: lakes, waterfalls, water towers, and, if our passing grade in high school chemistry is any indication, even hell.

Q Do farmers really need that extra hour of Daylight Saving Time?

A Sure, go and blame farmers because you lose a whole hour of sleep every spring. It's a common misconception that Daylight Saving Time (DST) was created to help farmers. The truth is, they're none too pleased about it either.

You see, cows and crops don't really care what the clock says. They're on "God's Time," otherwise known as Apparent Solar Time. When the sun's up, they're up. And when the clock is set an hour later, farmers lose a whole hour of morning productivity.

So if you can't point your tired little finger at the farmers, then who is responsible? Well, it was Benjamin Franklin who first proposed the idea of "saving daylight." While serving as the American delegate to France in 1784, he wrote an essay titled "An Economical Project for Diminishing the Cost of Light." In it, the thrifty Franklin discussed resetting clocks to make the most use of natural daylight hours. This, he said, could save Parisian families "an immense sum" per year in the cost of tallow and wax for evening candles.

Though many were intrigued (and amused) by Franklin's essay, the concept of daylight saving didn't take hold until more than a century later, when Englishman William Willett presented it again in his pamphlet "The Waste of Daylight" (1907). When World

War I began, the British Parliament enacted DST throughout England to reduce the need for artificial lighting and save fuel.

In 1918 the U.S. Congress followed suit, placing America on DST to conserve resources for the remainder of the war. Even back then, DST was widely unpopular. The law was repealed in 1919 and not observed again until WWII, when President Roosevelt instituted year-round DST, called "War Time," from 1942 to 1945.

From 1945 to 1966 there were no U.S. laws regarding DST. This meant that states and local towns were free to observe DST—or not. How did anyone know what time *Bonanza* was on? Suffice it to say, there was plenty of confusion.

Congress took action in 1966, enacting the Uniform Time Act to establish consistent timelines across the country. But any area that wanted to remain exempt from DST could do so by passing a local ordinance.

The Energy Policy Act of 2005 extended DST, beginning in 2007, to the time it is currently: It begins at 2:00 AM on the second Sunday in March and ends at 2:00 AM on the first Sunday in November. Proponents of DST say that it saves energy and prevents traffic accidents and crimes while providing extra daylight time for outdoor activities. Still, DST has its share of detractors.

The farming state of Indiana—one of the last states to adopt statewide DST, in April 2006—has fueled the DST debate. A 2007 study by Matthew Kotchen and Laura Grant of the University of Santa Barbara concluded that enacting DST in Indiana actually increased electricity consumption in the state, costing Indiana households an additional $8.6 million in 2007.

So, does DST conserve energy, as was originally intended? Well, it seems that DST has us turning off the evening lights but cranking up the AC. Inventive as he was, Benjamin Franklin never foresaw that.

Q Are the colors of the rainbow always in the same order?

A Yes. The order of the colors—red, orange, yellow, green, blue, indigo, and violet, from the top to the bottom—never changes. You may see a rainbow missing a color or two at its borders, but the visible colors always will be in the exact same order.

Rainbows are caused by the refraction of white light through a prism. In nature, water droplets in the air act as prisms. When light enters a prism, it is bent ever so slightly. The different wavelengths of light bend at different angles, so when white light hits a prism, it fans out. When the wavelengths are separated, the visible wavelengths appear as a rainbow.

The colors of a rainbow always appear in the same order because the wavelengths of the visible color spectrum always bend in the same way. They are ordered by the length of their waves. Red has the longest wavelength, about six hundred and fifty nanometers. Violet has the shortest, about four hundred nanometers. The other colors have wavelengths that fall between red and violet.

The human eye is incapable of seeing light that falls outside of these wavelengths. Light with a wavelength shorter than four hundred nanometers is invisible; we refer to it as ultraviolet light. Likewise, light with a wavelength longer than six hundred fifty nanometers cannot be seen; we call it infrared light.

Now, about that pot of gold at the end of a rainbow—how do you get to it? If we knew that, we'd have better things to do than answer these silly questions.

Q At what temperature does the weather qualify as hot?

A "But it's a dry heat." Civic-minded residents of the American Southwest say this phrase defensively to thick-blooded tourists from the Northeast and Midwest, and these tourists go home and repeat it sarcastically to their friends and family before busting out in gales of laughter.

To most people who don't spend much time in the desert heat, any temperature in excess of ninety degrees Fahrenheit is hot, and any temperature over one hundred is a reason to pine for the relative comfort of a ten-inch snowfall in February. But cooler heads prevail among the folks at the National Weather Service. They know that your ability to survive a one-hundred-degree day really does depend on how dry the heat is.

The human body dissipates heat in several ways, the most obvious being through perspiration. When your sweat hits the air, it turns to vapor. The energy required to fuel this process comes from the heat in your body, so the more vapor your sweat creates, the more heat you expend, and you get cooler. As the relative humidity rises, the air's ability to absorb moisture decreases. In other words, it don't need your stinkin' sweat because it's wet enough already. So the sweat just sits there on your skin, and now you're not only hot, you're also disgusting.

The National Weather Service uses a scale, called the heat index, to give us a better indication of levels of comfort and safety when it gets too darn hot. By combining the relative humidity with the air temperature, the heat index gives us what is called the "apparent temperature," which more accurately describes how hot you feel—rather than how hot it actually is—under the given conditions.

The National Weather Service divides heat-index readings into four levels to give people an idea of how dangerous the current heat-humidity combo is: Caution, Extreme Caution, Danger, and Extreme Danger. The higher the level, the more likely you are to develop heat-related health problems like heat cramps, heat exhaustion, and heat stroke. When the temperature is ninety degrees and the relative humidity is just 5 percent, for example, the heat index is on the cusp between the lowest two ratings, Caution and Extreme Caution. If the humidity is 95 percent, however, that ninety-degree temperature results in a heat index of over 130 degrees, placing it in the Extreme Danger range.

This is valuable information, to be sure. While tornadoes, hurricanes, and lightning storms make for sexy TV images, heat kills more people in the United States than all other types of weather disasters combined—and the heat index is the best way to gauge just how disastrous a hot day can be. So don't laugh at the good folks in the American Southwest. A dry heat really is more comfortable.

Q Do rivers always flow north to south?

A No, rivers are not subject to any natural laws that compel them to flow north to south. Only one thing governs the direction of a river's flow: gravity.

Quite simply, every river travels from points of higher elevation to points of lower elevation. Most rivers originate in mountains, hills, or other highlands. From there, it's always a long and winding journey to sea level.

Many prominent rivers flow from north to south, which perhaps creates the misconception that all waterways do so. The Mississippi River and its tributaries flow in a southerly direction as they make their way to the Gulf of Mexico. The Colorado River runs south toward the Gulf of California, and the Rio Grande follows a mostly southerly path.

But there are many major rivers that do not flow north to south. The Amazon flows northeast, and both the Nile and the Rhine head north. The Congo River flaunts convention entirely by flowing almost due north, then cutting a wide corner and going south toward the Atlantic Ocean.

There's a tendency to think of north and south as up and down. This comes from the mapmaking convention of sketching the world with the North Pole at the top of the illustration and the South Pole at the bottom.

But rivers don't follow the conventions of mapmakers. They're downhill racers that will go anywhere gravity takes them.

Q How deep are the oceans?

A First, the boring answer. Going by average depth, the Pacific Ocean is the deepest: 13,740 feet. The Indian and Atlantic oceans are a close second and third at 12,740 and 12,254 feet deep, respectively. The Arctic Ocean is relatively shallow— 3,407 feet at its deepest point.

But there's much more to the story. The terrain of the land that lies beneath the oceans is just as varied as the terrain of the higher and drier parts of the globe. The ocean floors have their own mountain ranges—the tallest of which poke through the waves to become islands—and they also have plunging valleys called trenches.

These trenches mark the seams at which two of the earth's tectonic plates come together; movement of these plates forces one under the other in a process called subduction. Trenches can be narrow, but they run the entire lengths of the tectonic plates.

Trenches are the deepest parts of the oceans—and the deepest of all the trenches is the Mariana Trench, which is named for its proximity to the Mariana Islands, which are located in the Pacific Ocean between Australia and Japan. The depth of the Mariana Trench varies considerably along its 1,580 miles, but oceanographers have identified one part that's deeper than the others—in other words, the deepest part of the deepest trench in the deepest ocean on the planet. This place is called the Challenger Deep.

The bottom of this valley in the ocean floor is a bone-crushing 35,810 feet deep—almost seven miles below sea level. One way to illustrate this depth is to say that if we wanted to hide Mount Everest—the entire thing—they could toss it into the Challenger Deep. Once it had settled on the bottom, there would still be more than a mile of water between the highest point of the mountain and the ocean's surface.

The Challenger Deep, discovered in 1951, was named for the first vessel to pinpoint the deepest part of the trench: HMS *Challenger II,* manned by Jacques Piccard. The first vessel to plumb these depths was the U.S. Naval submersible *Trieste* in 1960, manned by Piccard and U.S. Navy Lt. Don Walsh. Hydrostatic pressure, caused by the accumulated weight of the water above you, increases as you descend into a body of water. At the bottom of the Challenger Deep, the *Trieste* had to withstand eight tons of pressure per square inch. Bone-crushing, indeed.

Q Can you be killed by a plant?

A The good news is, unless you're a character in *Little Shop of Horrors,* no plant is going to kill you with malicious intent or for food.

That doesn't mean you shouldn't fear death by plant. Obviously, a tree could fall on you or twist your car into a pretzel if you veer off the road. But the more gruesome scenarios involve eating something you shouldn't. Here's a sampling from the menu of green meanies:

- Aconitum (aconite, monkshood, or wolfsbane) will start your mouth burning from the first nibble. Then you'll start vomiting, your lungs and heart will shut down, and you'll die of asphyxiation. As luck would have it, your mind will stay alert the entire time. And you don't even have to eat aconitum to enjoy its effects: Just brush up against it and the sap can get through your skin.

- Hemlock is another particularly nasty snack. In fact, the ancient Greeks gave it to prisoners who were condemned to die (including Socrates). Ingest some hemlock and it will eventually paralyze your nervous system, causing you to die from lack of oxygen to the brain and heart. Fortunately, if you happen to have an artificial ventilation system nearby, you can hook yourself up and wait about three days for the effects to wear off. But even if there is a ventilation system handy, it's best if you just don't eat hemlock.

- Oleander is chock full of poisony goodness, too. Every part of these lovely ornamental plants is deadly if ingested. Just one leaf can be fatal to a small child, while adults might get to enjoy up to ten leaves before venturing into the big sleep. Even its fumes are toxic—never use Oleander branches as firewood. Oleander poisoning will affect most parts of your body: the central nervous system, the skin, the heart, and the brain. After the seizures and the tremors, you may welcome the sweet relief of the coma that might come next. Unfortunately, that can be followed by death.

So, while there is no need to worry about any plants sneaking up on you from behind with a baseball bat, there are plenty of reasons not to take a nibble out of every plant you see.

Q How long is a day on Mars?

A The Martian solar day lasts about twenty-four hours and forty minutes. That's not much longer than a day on Earth, but it would give Earthlings who might eventually colonize the red planet a substantial advantage. Think about how much more you could accomplish with an extra forty minutes per day. It would amount to about an extra twenty hours per month.

Those colonists would need to adjust their calendar as well as their clock. A year on Mars is about 687 Earth days. This is because Mars has a much longer path of orbit around the sun. Earth zips around the sun almost twice before Mars completes one full circuit.

Because of its extended path of orbit, Mars experiences four seasons that last twice as long as those on Earth. Spring and summer are almost two hundred days each; fall and winter are about one hundred and fifty days each. Martian farmers would have a lot of time to plant and harvest, but they'd also have to conserve that harvest through a much longer, much harsher winter.

Everything lasts longer on Mars than on Earth. For those colonists, the Martian work week would be an extra three hours and twenty minutes, and the weekend would be extended by an hour and twenty minutes. Summer vacation would be long, but the school year would be longer still.

A blessing or a curse? Depends on what you're doing with your extra forty minutes per day.

Q What's the difference between a star and a planet?

A Even astronomers quibble over this one. In the most general terms, stars and planets can be differentiated by two characteristics: what they're made of and whether they produce their own light. According to the Space Telescope Science Institute, a star is "a huge ball of gas held together by gravity." At its core, this huge ball of gas is super-hot. It's so hot that a star produces enough energy to twinkle and glow. You know, "like a diamond in the sky."

In case you didn't know, our own sun is a star. The light and energy it produces are enough to sustain life on Earth. But compared to other stars, the sun is only average in temperature and size. Talk about star power! It's no wonder that crazed teenage girls and planets revolve around stars. In fact, the word "planet" is derived from the Greek *plan te* ("wanderer"). By definition, planets are objects that orbit around stars. As for composition, planets are made up mostly of rock (Earth, Mercury, Venus, and Mars) or gas (Jupiter, Saturn, Neptune, and Uranus).

Now hold your horoscopes! If planets can be gaseous, then just what makes Uranus different from the stars that form Ursa Major?

Well, unlike stars, planets are built around solid cores. They're cooler in temperature, and some are even home to water and ice. Remember what the planet Krypton looked like in the *Superman* movies? All right, so glacial Krypton is not a real planet, but you get the point: Gaseous planets aren't hot enough to produce their own light. They may appear to be shining, but they're actually only reflecting the light of their suns.

So back to the astronomers: Just what are they quibbling about? Well, it's tough agreeing on exact definitions for stars and planets when there are a few celestial objects that fall somewhere in between the two. Case in point: brown dwarfs.

Brown dwarfs are too small and cool to produce their own light, so they can't be considered stars. Yet they seem to form in the same way stars do, and since they have gaseous cores, they can't be considered planets either. So what to call brown dwarfs? Some say "failed stars," "substars," or even "planetars." In our vast universe, there seems to be plenty of room for ambiguity.

Chapter Twelve

SPORTS

Q Does a curveball really curve?

A The curveball has been baffling hitters for well more than a hundred years. Hall-of-Famer William "Candy" Cummings is credited with being the first pitcher to master the curve, which he began throwing with great success in 1867 as a member of the Brooklyn Excelsiors. Anyone who has stood in a batter's box and faced a pitcher with an effective curve will tell you that the ball is definitely doing something unusual.

Yet for almost as long as pitchers have been buckling batters' knees with the breaking ball, a small contingent of naysayers has maintained that the ball does not curve, that the whole thing is an optical illusion. Before the availability of advanced photographic technology, various tests were occasionally performed by those curious enough to want to know the truth. Pitchers threw curveballs around boards, through hoops, and parallel to long rods. In 1941, *Life* magazine did a photographic analysis of a curveball and concluded that, no, the ball does not actually curve. The same year, however, *Look* magazine did its own tests and came to the opposite conclusion.

Today's super-slow-motion TV technology catch curveballs in the act all the time, and it sure looks like the ball is curving. And the truth is, a curveball does curve. Physicists have said so, decisively. They can even tell you the name of the principle that makes it curve: the Magnus effect.

A pitcher who throws a curveball snaps his wrist when he throws, creating a high rate of topspin on the ball. As the ball travels, the air passing on the side against the spin creates drag and higher pressure, while the air passing on the other side has no drag and the pressure is lower. The higher air pressure on one side effectively pushes the ball toward the low-pressure side, sometimes a foot or more. That's the Magnus effect.

The force of gravity also comes into play. Because a curveball is thrown at a slower rate of speed than a fastball, the curve will drop more noticeably than a fastball as it approaches the batter. The combination of the curve and the drop makes it difficult to predict where the ball will be once it reaches home plate and, thus, confounding to hit.

There's even an equation to figure out how much a ball will curve. It looks like this: $F\text{Magnus Force} = KwVCv$. This may seem complicated, but we're willing to bet that for most people, it's still easier to solve the curveball equation than it is to hit the curveball.

Q Which sport has the greatest athletes?

A Sometimes the simplest questions are the most complicated to answer. Even if you agree on the criteria for which sport has the greatest athletes—strength, agility, endurance, coordination, all of the above, or some of the above—you come up with no consensus on the answer. So let's start by running down some of the experts' opinions.

Canada's Sun Media newspapers published a series of articles in 2007 in which five sports were analyzed—basketball, baseball, football, hockey, and soccer—and the arguments for soccer players being the greatest athletes seemed the most persuasive. Soccer players run six miles or more per game, combining jogging and sprinting for ninety minutes. There are changes of direction, vertical jumps, astounding acts of agility, one-on-one battles that often get physical, and the need to be just as sharp in the nineti-eth minute as in the first. The writer called soccer the most physically demanding team sport.

However, Sun Media's own medical expert, Dr. Bob Litchfield, medical director of the Fowler Kennedy Sports Medicine Clinic at the University of Western Ontario, cast his vote for basketball because of the wear and tear players in that sport—particularly NBA guards—must endure.

When the scope is widened beyond major sports, other athletes make powerful cases. The *St. Petersburg Times* in Florida did research in 2004 and decided the toughest sport is—drum roll, please—water polo. Sorry, but there's something anticlimactic about that one. For another perspective, the *Times* talked to Dr. Peter Davis, director of coaching and sports sciences for the United States Olympic Committee (USOC). Davis presumably has the kind of broad-based practical experience necessary to render an objective answer. "My vote for world's best athlete? I'd say an Australian Rules football player," Davis said. "Then again, I'm biased. I'm from Australia."

Davis also pointed out that in winning the Tour de France—and doing so seven times in a row, we might add—Lance Armstrong accomplished the equivalent of running a marathon every day or two for a month. Davis further noted that USOC scientists consider synchronized swimming the most grueling sport. "Try treading water for a minute while making perfectly choreographed movements. And, oh yeah, do it upside down, under water," he said.

Men's Journal magazine did its top ten in 2003 and decided on gymnastics, followed by the Ironman triathlon, rock climbing, hockey, bull riding, boxing, rugby, decathlon, water polo, and football. No soccer, basketball, Australian Rules football, endurance bicycling, or synchronized swimming. See how hard it is to find a consensus? Then there are the oh-so-clever pundits who claim that racehorses are the best athletes. Yes, they're powerful, graceful, and fast. But have you ever seen a horse hit a curveball?

As you can see, the answer to this question is completely subjective. Our vote goes for basketball, which combines all of soccer's strength and agility needs with most of its endurance demands, then layers on the whole upper-body thing plus equal or greater degrees of physical contact. Then again, we could just throw up our hands and vote for poker players. After all, they have to worry about hemorrhoids. And those things are painful.

Q Do you have to be fat to be a sumo wrestler?

A In other words, can you be thin and compete in sumo? Not since George Carlin's comedy rant on the English language's oxymoronic couplets ("jumbo shrimp," "military intelligence") has there been a more mismatched concept than "thin" and "sumo." With good reason.

Historically, these supersize athletes *(rikishis)* have been known to dent the scales from roughly 220 pounds, which would comprise the sport's version of a 98-pound weakling, to 518 pounds. But in the world of professional sumo—with its incessant hand-slapping, salt-tossing, foot-stomping, bull-rushing, and chest-bashing—big isn't universally or undeniably better.

In the traditional ranks of Japanese sumo, where kudos to Shinto deities to ensure healthy harvests once played as large a role as blubber-to-blubber combat, the highest order of achievers are given the honorable title *yokozuna*. (No, *yokozuna* does not translate to "Is there any more cake?")

To become a *yokozuna,* a wrestler must simultaneously satisfy both subjective and objective criteria. He must dominate in the *dohyo,* or ring, where two consecutive Grand Tournament wins are considered a nifty way to attract the eye of Japan Sumo Association judges. He also must demonstrate a combination of skill, power, dignity, and grace. Fewer than seventy men in the centuries-old sport of sumo have ascended to this lofty tier, and most have been larger-than-life figures—literally.

The twenty-seventh *yokozuna,* known as Tochigiyama, was an exception. A star of the sport between 1918 and 1925, Tochigiyama was a comparative beanpole, at about 230 pounds. Yet he proved to be a crafty tactician, frequently moving mountains...of flesh. His won-loss record was 115–8.

At the opposite end of the spectrum loomed the mighty Musashimaru, the sixty-seventh *yokozuna.* He dominated the eighteen-square-foot *dohyo* while clad in his *mawashi* (not a diaper, though it looks like one) between 1999 and 2003. Musashimaru won about 75 percent of his three hundred or so bouts, due in great measure to the fearsome nature of his physique. He tipped the scales at about 520 pounds, give or take a sack of bacon cheeseburgers.

Somewhere in the middle, we find perhaps the greatest of them

all: Taiho, who reigned in the 1960s and became the forty-eighth *yokozuna.* Taiho chalked up thirty-two tournament wins and weighed 337 pounds.

So here's the skinny on sumo wrestling: You don't have to be fat to do it.

Q How did the term "bogey" find its way into golf?

A All sorts of golf terms have fuzzy histories. This is hardly surprising, since the game is more than five hundred years old and is generally accepted to have begun with a gang of Scots whacking the ball across sheep pastures.

Amazingly enough, we not only can pin down the time that the word "bogey" was brought into play in golf, but we can also cite the specific place. The odd wrinkle, though, is that the story behind the term seems to depend on which side of the pond you're on, and the origin of the word itself is unknown. By the way, when the term came into use, a "bogey" meant what golfers now call "par."

According to the British Golf Museum, "bogey" originated from "the mythical golfer, Colonel Bogey, a player of high amateur standard who was held to play every hole of a given course in the standard stroke score." The version of events given by the United States Golf Association (USGA) says that the term comes from "a song that was popular in the British Isles in the early 1890s." Whether the ruling body of golf in America knows more about the gent known as Bogey than the folks who are thought to have invented golf is open to debate (perhaps they are both correct), but there is agreement on both sides of the Atlantic about when and where the term and the sport got together.

The use of the term "bogey" in golf began in Norfolk, England, around 1890. The Great Yarmouth Golf Club adopted a suggestion from Hugh Rotherham, secretary of the Coventry Golf Club, that there should be a standard to judge the number of shots a good golfer ought to score on any given hole that did not rely on the score of one's opponents. For centuries, golf scoring was based on match play—all that mattered was that a golfer's score per hole was lower than the opponent's. Later, in the mid-seventeen hundreds, the total number of strokes were counted but were still compared to the scores of other players. Rotherham's fixed score, which he called a "ground score," was accepted and then put into use.

Golfing authority Robert Browning, editor of *Golfing* magazine for forty-five years, reports that as Dr. Thomas Brown, honorary secretary of the Great Yarmouth Club, was explaining the new ground score concept to a friend, the friend joked that the imaginary opponent was a "regular boogey man." Some speculate that Dr. Browne's friend was influenced by a newly popular song of the time whose refrain was, "Hush! hush! hush! Here comes the bogey man."

The USGA says the song was "The Bogey Man" and later was known as "The Colonel Bogey March." However, that latter musical piece was not published until 1914, although its title is connected with one of the composer's golfing experiences. According to author Browning, during another introduction of this new fashion of scoring to the honorary secretary of another golfing club in spring 1892, it was suggested that "nothing less than the rank of Colonel would befit the dignity of a player so steady and accurate."

Other golfers picked up the term—meaning it as a compliment—and soon enough "ground score" was replaced in common usage by the word "bogey." Players then considered themselves matched against the mythical Colonel Bogey.

As golfers got better and scores started dropping early in the twentieth century, all professionals and the top amateur players began shooting scores well under the established bogey numbers still in use at most British courses. In 1911, the USGA adopted exact distances for determining what it called "par" on all holes, and suddenly bogey wasn't so good, as the meaning switched to one stroke over par.

In a slightly embarrassing snippet of history for the home of golf, Britain didn't join the move to par until 1925. Thus "bogey" became a stroke over par worldwide—a fist pump or a club slammed to the ground, depending on a player's skill level.

Q What's the difference between billiards and pool?

A It's a trick question: There is no difference. Billiards is a catchall term that includes a number of games that are played on a rectangular, felt-topped table and involve hitting balls with a long stick (the cue). Some of the more popular games include French (or carom) billiards, English billiards, snooker, and pocket billiards (which is the game you know as pool).

If you're a pool player accustomed to the satisfying clunk of a ball dropping into one of the pockets, French billiards will probably make you feel like you're in that weird, abstract foreign film that you were forced to watch on a bad date. There are no pockets, and there are only three balls: one white; one red; and one either yellow or white, with a little red dot on it. Either of the white balls (or the yellow ball) can serve as the cue ball. The point of the game is for the cue ball to hit the other two balls in succession. This is a carom. Each time a carom is accomplished, a point is awarded. The player who manages to keep from dying of boredom the longest is the winner.

English billiards incorporates the same three balls as French billiards, but the table has the six pockets familiar to pool players—one in each corner, and one on each of the long sides of the rectangle. There are four ways to score: You can hit the two balls in succession, à la French billiards; you can hit the red ball into a pocket; you can hit the other cue ball into a pocket; or you can hit the cue ball against another ball before the cue ball goes into a pocket. The winner is the player who can tally the score without using a slide rule.

Snooker also is played on a table with six pockets, but there are twenty-two balls: fifteen red balls, six balls of various colors that are assigned numbers, and a cue ball. After you knock a red ball into a pocket, you're allowed to pocket one of the numbered balls. The ball's number is added to your score, and then the ball is returned to the table. Then you have to pocket another red ball before going after a numbered ball, and so on. The winner is the player who can go the longest without giggling at any mention of the word "snooker."

Pocket billiards, or pool, involves fifteen numbered balls and a cue ball. Pool is played in bars, bowling alleys, and basement rec rooms across North America by people in various states of inebriation. Popular variations of pool include the games rotation, straight pool, and eight ball. Scoring systems differ, but the point of each game ultimately is to avoid finger injuries between games, when angry, drunken losing players engage in the time-honored tradition of venting their frustrations by hitting the remaining balls way harder than anyone would ever need to hit them.

Q Why do baseball fans stretch in the seventh inning?

A Presidents of the United States have long had a connection to America's national pastime. Ronald Reagan famously recreated the play-by-play of Chicago Cubs games without watching any of the action (preparing him quite nicely, some say, for his presidency). George W. Bush was part-owner of the Texas Rangers for nearly a decade, becoming a managing partner thanks to his oil-company pals (preparing him quite nicely, some say, for his presidency). And Opening Day wouldn't be complete without the sitting president awkwardly throwing out the first pitch, a tradition started in 1910 by William Howard Taft in a game between the Washington Senators and Philadelphia Athletics.

According to baseball folklore—of which there is a seemingly endless amount—it was the portly, peace-loving Taft who also started the tradition of the seventh-inning stretch at that same Opening Day game in 1910. As the tale goes, Taft, who was a baseball fanatic (and a promising catcher before embarking upon a political career), rose to stretch his corpulent frame after the top of the seventh inning. The crowd, believing Taft was departing, rose in respect for its commander-in-chief, only to somewhat confusedly sit back down when Taft returned to his seat as the bottom of the inning commenced. Thus, the seventh-inning stretch was born.

Like many apocryphal tales, the story of Taft inventing the seventh-inning stretch is dubious. Indeed, the practice of fans stretching in the middle of the seventh inning goes back to at least 1869. In that year, Harry Wright, the manager of the Cincinnati Red Stockings, wrote a letter to a friend in which he claimed "the spectators all arise between halves of the seventh inning, extend their legs and arms." That sounds suspiciously like a stretch, doesn't it? There is no record as to why this tradition existed, though the hard wooden benches of the grandstand might provide a cogent explanation.

Nowadays, the seventh-inning stretch is entrenched in baseball tradition and often features the crowd singing along to the traditional "Take Me Out to the Ball Game" (or in polka-loving Milwaukee, "Roll Out the Barrel"). Of course, with the modern trend of baseball stadiums cutting off alcohol sales after the seventh inning, the seventh-inning stretch has turned into more of a seventh-inning sprint—to the beer stand.

Q Has dwarf tossing been banned in every state?

A Life was simpler back in the 1980s. It was "Morning in America again," according to President Reagan. Director John Hughes tugged at our heartstrings with movies that exposed the hardship of being sixteen, misunderstood, and rich. And dwarf tossing was in its heyday.

Indeed, the phenomenon took flight during the mid-1980s in Australia and the United States. Ostensibly a competitive endeavor, it involved an average-size person picking up a dwarf and tossing him as far as possible into some sort of landing pit, which often consisted of mattresses. Participating dwarfs made themselves more tossable by wearing padding and a harness with strategically placed handles. Cash prizes were awarded for the longest tosses.

Like loud, pointless arguments and regrettable sexual encounters, dwarf tossing appealed mainly to the inebriated, and so the competitions always took place in bars.

As dwarf tossing grew in popularity, so did the controversy surrounding it. In 1985, Chicago Mayor Harold Washington called it "degrading and mean-spirited," and the city successfully scuttled a dwarf-tossing competition by threatening to revoke the liquor license of the host bar. Other communities employed similar preventive tactics. While promoters and their fearless flying dwarfs argued for the right to earn a living, opponents cited safety concerns and the objectification of little people.

The turning point came in 1989. As the good-time 1980s prepared to give way to the politically correct 1990s, an organization called Little People of America lobbied successfully for legislation outlawing dwarf tossing in Florida. New York followed suit, and soon the dwarf toss had joined Atari, Cabbage Patch kids, and Duran Duran on the scrap heap of 1980s pop culture.

European nations issued their own prohibitions throughout the 1990s. Even the United Nations and its Human Rights Committee got involved, upholding in 2002 France's dwarf-tossing ban after it was challenged by three-foot, ten-inch Manuel Wackenheim, who said the ban kept him from earning a living.

Is it banned in every U.S. state? Hardly. Technically, it's not even banned in Florida, the Ground Zero of dwarf tossing. That was made clear in 2001 when a three-foot, two-inch radio personality named Dave "The Dwarf" Flood hired a lawyer and tried to overturn the state's anti-dwarf-tossing law.

At issue was the specific stipulation against dwarf tossing in bars. If you get the urge to fling a consenting dwarf in the Sunshine State, nobody can stop you—unless you do it in a drinking establishment, in which case the bar will lose its liquor license and be fined up to one thousand dollars.

As Flood knew, few people other than bar drunks are interested in watching dwarf tossing. Florida's law, he argued, violated his rights under the U.S. Constitution. Can you guess what happened when Flood filed his lawsuit in U.S. District Court? Yup, the judge tossed it out of court.

Q How come a hockey puck is so hard to follow?

A If you have trouble following a hockey puck as it darts all over the ice, you're probably relatively new to the sport. Spectators who are indoctrinated enough to have lost a tooth or two in the stands—or at their local watering holes—during heated arguments about their favorite hockey teams have little trouble tracking that black blur, mostly because they can anticipate the action.

Hockey bills itself as the fastest sport around, and not just because of the puck. True, in the National Hockey League (NHL), a great scorer's slap shot can easily top one hundred miles per hour—in the 1960s, Chicago Blackhawks star Bobby Hull had a slap shot clocked at 120 miles per hour and a wrist shot of 105 miles per hour.

The players themselves are a blur, too. They skate at thirty miles per hour in sprinting situations and at twenty miles per hour when they're cruising down the ice. Such speed is rarely seen in the "foot" team sports, such as football, basketball, and baseball. So the frenetic action around the puck is part of what makes that black disc so hard to follow.

Still, the puck isn't completely innocent in this. At one inch thick and three inches wide, it's much smaller than a football or basketball. Hockey fans learn to keep tabs on the puck as they pick up on the nuances of the sport. They anticipate charges down the ice and take notice of how players position themselves for scoring opportunities, and they grow to appreciate the "nonpuck" plays, like checking and boxing out.

Watching hockey on television can be a challenge, and the Fox network tried to help with its use of the "smart puck" in the mid-1990s. Fox used the wonders of modern technology to transform the puck into a colored dot that had an easy-to-follow trail. The smart puck was widely panned for its distracting and bastardizing effect on the games. In fact, the only thing smart about it was that it went into cold storage after Fox's TV contract with the NHL expired. But the smart puck did have some value. It taught us that sometimes harder is better.

Q In soccer, why are yellow cards yellow and red cards red?

A Considering that soccer has existed in its modern form since the mid-nineteenth century, it's rather strange that no formal penalty system—i.e., red cards and yellow cards—was put into place until the latter part of the twentieth century.

The situation is stranger still when you consider the innocuous way in which red cards and yellow cards came to be. Ken Aston, a headmaster at a British school, was sitting at a stoplight after attending a World Cup quarterfinal between England and Argentina in 1966 when an idea that would change soccer popped into his head. "As I drove down Kensington High Street, the traffic light turned red," Aston said. "I thought, 'Yellow, take it easy; red, stop, you're off.'"

Aston's brainstorm was prompted by the lack of formal, announced penalties in soccer at the time. As ridiculous as it seems, players could be penalized in a soccer match or ejected without any sort of declaration from the referee. In the England versus Argentina match, numerous players had been ejected by the referee without being told of their infraction. Aston knew the obvious: Soccer needed a formalized way to keep players and fans informed of infractions.

The global soccer community embraced Aston's idea. The system of yellow and red cards was adopted in time for the 1970 World Cup in Mexico City. For those who don't follow soccer closely, here is a quick tutorial on why a ref would pull out a yellow card or red card.

A yellow card is presented to a player as a warning after any of the following infractions:

- Unsportsmanlike conduct
- Dissent by word or actions
- Persistent rule-breaking
- Delaying the restart of play
- Defending a corner kick or free kick too closely
- Entering or leaving the field without referee permission

A red card is given if a player receives two yellow cards in a match, or when any of the following occurs:

- Serious foul play
- Violence
- Spitting
- Denying an obvious goal-scoring opportunity by deliberately handling the ball
- Fouling an opponent to prevent an obvious goal-scoring opportunity
- Offensive or threatening language

If shown a red card, a player is "sent off" and cannot be replaced, forcing his or her team to compete one player short.

Since Aston's epiphany, the practice of issuing colored cards has been adopted by other sports besides soccer, including volleyball, rugby, field hockey, lacrosse, and handball. In rugby, a yellow card gets you sent to the "sin bin," which is like the penalty box in hockey.

In soccer, a yellow gets you a break from the game. It sounds genteel enough, just as Aston imagined it while idling at that traffic light. The reality, however, has been something different, especially in soccer-crazed Europe. Sometimes an ill-issued yellow card can spark a near-riot, which begs the question: Why doesn't soccer have a "sin bin," too...for its hooligan fans?

Chapter Thirteen

MORE GOOD STUFF

Q **Are men bigger tightwads than women?**

A How old is the car you drive? How long are your showers? At what temperature do you keep your home in winter?

These are just a few questions from the official Tightwad-Spend-thrift Survey, an international research study that was conducted by behavioral economists Scott Rick of The Wharton School of the University of Pennsylvania, and Cynthia Cryder and George Loewenstein of Carnegie Mellon University.

After surveying more than thirteen thousand shoppers worldwide, these researchers surmised that being a tightwad goes way beyond being economically frugal. And they discovered that, yes, one gender is indeed less likely to be generous in its spending habits.

Frugal people take pleasure in saving money. They clip coupons or buy all their Christmas decorations on December 26. No biggie. These prudent purchasers tend to be happy folks.

You can't say as much for tightwads. According to the study, those who fall into the tightwad category are less happy with life. (Ever heard of a guy named Scrooge?) For tightwads, forking over a five is like dying a little death. It's an emotionally painful experience they'll relive again and again. Tightwads aren't pinching pennies out of concern for the future: Instead, they forgo purchasing necessities or things that would genuinely improve their lives, even though they can well afford them.

They save pails of cloudy bathwater to wash their clothes or water plants. They reuse coffee grounds and tea bags at least three times. They hang wet paper towels out to dry, cut up Twinkie boxes to make postcards, and order drive-through burgers without cheese because they've got cheese at home.

And most of these misers are men.

Responses from the Tightwad-Spendthrift Survey, published in the *Journal of Consumer Research* in April 2008, reveal that females are no more likely to be tightwads than they are to be big spenders. Males, on the other hand, are almost three times more likely to be tightwads than big spenders.

To make matters worse, tightwaddism seems exacerbated by age. Those older than seventy are five times more likely to be tightwads than spendthrifts. Maybe this helps explain why Grandpa hangs his dental floss over the towel rack so that he can use it again tomorrow.

Q How can celebrity tabloids get away with publishing obviously untrue stories?

A Supermarket tabloids thrive on publishing outlandish celebrity rumors and innuendo. You'd think that the subjects of their articles would be suing them all the time. How in the world could the tabloids survive the legal fees and multimillion-dollar judgments? The truth is, if tabloids are good at one thing, it's surviving.

There are two kinds of tabloids: the ridiculous that publish stories no one really believes ("Bigfoot Cured My Arthritis!") and those that focus on celebrity gossip.

The ridiculous stories are easy to get away with. They're mostly fabricated or based on slender truths. As long as they contain nothing damaging about a real person, there's no one to file a lawsuit. Bigfoot isn't litigious.

Celebrity gossip is trickier. To understand how tabloids avoid legal problems, we need to learn a little bit about the legal definition of libel. To be found guilty of libel, you must have published something about another person that is provably false.

Moreover, the falsehood has to have caused that person some kind of damage, even if only his or her reputation is harmed. If the subject of the story is a notable person, such as a politician or a movie star, libel legally occurs only if publication of the falsehood was malicious. This means that the publisher knew the information was false, had access to the truth but ignored it, and published the information anyway.

Tabloids generally have lawyers on staff or on retainer who are experts in media law and libel. By consulting with their lawyers, tabloid editors can publish stories that get dangerously close to libel but don't quite cross the line.

One defense against libel is publication of the truth: You can't sue someone for saying something about you that's true, no matter how embarrassing it may be. And tabloids know that if they print something close to the truth, a celebrity is unlikely to sue because a trial could reveal a skeleton in the closet that's even more embarrassing.

Libel lawyers also know that a tabloid is in the clear if it publishes a story based on an informant's opinion. Opinions can't be disproved, so they don't meet the criteria for libel. This explains headlines such as this: "Former Housekeeper Says Movie Star Joe Smith Is a Raving Lunatic!" As long as the tabloid makes a token effort to corroborate the story—or even includes a rebuttal of the housekeeper's claims within the article—it is fairly safe from a legal standpoint.

Of course, legal tricks don't always work. Some movie stars, musicians, and other celebrities have successfully sued tabloids for tens of millions of dollars. That tabloids continue to thrive despite such judgments shows just how much money there is to be made in the rumors-and-innuendo business.

Q How crazy do you have to be to be considered legally insane?

A No, judges don't keep a "You must be *this* nuts to get out of jail" sign hidden behind their benches. But you can be found not guilty by reason of insanity if you're cuckoo in just the right way.

Criminal insanity doesn't refer to any specific mental disorder, but it is related to mental illness. The reasoning behind the insanity defense is that some mental disorders may cause people to lose the ability to understand their actions or to differentiate between right and wrong, leaving them unable to truly have criminal intent. Intent is an important element of crime. If you intentionally burn down a house by dropping a lit cigarette in a trash can, we'd call you an arsonist. But if you do exactly the same thing accidentally, we'd probably just call you an inconsiderate (and perhaps a criminally negligent) jerk.

Similarly, the reasoning goes, you shouldn't be punished if a mental illness leads you to break the law without really comprehending your actions. Now, this doesn't apply to just any run-of-the-mill murderer with an antisocial personality disorder. A lack of empathy may lead someone to commit crimes, but if he understands what he's doing and he realizes that what he's doing is wrong, he's not insane.

You can only be found not guilty by reason of insanity in two cases: if mental illness keeps you from understanding your actions and deprives you of the ability to tell right from wrong, or if mental illness leaves you unable to control your actions and you experience an irresistible impulse to commit a crime. Details vary from state to state (and some states don't recognize the insanity defense at all), but these are the general criteria.

Some form of the insanity defense seems to date back to the sixteenth century, but early versions were awfully hazy. The 1843 trial of Daniel M'Naghten helped to clear things up. Thinking that the pope and English Prime Minister Robert Peel were out to get him, M'Naghten went to 10 Downing Street to kill Peel but ended up killing Peel's secretary. Witnesses claimed that M'Naghten was delusional, and the jury found him not guilty by reason of insanity. Queen Victoria was none too pleased, so a panel of judges was convened to clarify the rules governing the insanity defense as it involved the inability to distinguish right from wrong.

The definition has been controversial ever since, and every high-profile case seems to throw the idea into question. Patty Hearst and Jeffery Dahmer both tried to use the insanity defense unsuccessfully, while David Berkowitz (Son of Sam) and Ted Kaczynski (the Unabomber) seemed ready to pursue the defense but ultimately decided against it. But a jury did acquit John Hinckley Jr. of all charges related to his assassination attempt on President Reagan after it determined that he was insane.

A successful insanity plea is rare. In the 1990s, a study funded by the National Institute of Mental Health found that defendants pleaded insanity in less than 1 percent of cases, and that only a quarter of those pleas were successful. Those who are successful hardly ever get off scot-free. They're simply committed to mental institutions rather than sent to prisons; on average, those who are found insane end up spending more time confined to an institution than they would have in prison if they had been found guilty.

So unless you really love padded rooms, it's probably best to try another defense.

Q What makes diamonds so valuable?

A Ah, the curious case of the diamond. Although this isn't exactly a rags-to-riches story—gemstone-quality diamonds have always been prized—it is stunning just the same. Pearls, rubies, sapphires, and emeralds were all more valuable than diamonds at the beginning of the twentieth century, but not anymore. Why? Two words: De Beers.

Founded by South African businessman Cecil Rhodes in 1888, the De Beers cartel of companies controls nearly all aspects of diamond mining, transporting, cutting, and retailing all over the world. Marketing helped De Beers push the diamond over the top. In 1948 De Beers unveiled a slogan—"A Diamond Is Forever"—that created an inexorable link between the diamond and the promise of eternal love. And eternal love is priceless, right?

Since this masterstroke, which made the diamond a standard part of weddings, De Beers has created the eternity ring (a second chance to say that your love is forever), the trilogy ring (representing the past and the present, in addition to that eternal future), and the right-hand ring (for the woman who doesn't need a man and can find eternal love within herself).

To some degree, effective marketing has trumped the laws of supply and demand. Typically, something rises in value if there is low supply and increased demand, yet diamonds aren't particularly rare. In fact, the worldwide supply of the stones increased significantly in the twentieth century, due to improved mining techniques and the discovery of massive diamond deposits. Of course, not all diamonds are created equal—unlike precious metals, there is no universal price for diamonds based on weight. Diamonds that are superior in the four C's—color, clarity, cut, and carat weight—will fetch a greater sum of money than more run-of-the-mill stones.

The diamond trade has spurred funded wars in Africa, and in December 2000 the United Nations passed a resolution denouncing "conflict diamonds" or "blood diamonds"—those that are mined in territories controlled by governments or groups not recognized by the UN. (A legitimate diamond's provenance can be ascertained by its paperwork or sometimes by a small marking made by the cutter that can't be seen by the naked eye.) The 2006 film *Blood Diamond* brought even more attention to the human rights violations associated with diamond mining in African war zones.

Is a diamond forever? Forever is a very long time. Just to play it safe, you may want to pull Grandma's old pearls out of the jewelry box.

Q Are nickels made of nickel?

A What do you think they're made of, wood? The original U.S. five-cent piece was made of silver, at a time when all coins were required by law to be made of gold, silver, or copper. That silver five-cent piece was called a "half disme." ("Disme" was pronounced "dime." This was at a time, apparently, when some coins were required by law to have odd, confusingly spelled names.)

Congress—in its continuing, highly successful effort to cause confusion, create waste, and operate with an overall lack of efficiency—ordered the U.S. Mint to begin producing a new five-cent piece in 1866, although production of the now fully dissed half disme continued for another seven years. Made from nickel and copper, this new five-cent coin was significantly larger than the half disme, because nickel was relatively cheap compared to silver. Congress immediately dubbed the new coin the "nisckel." (Okay, we made up that last part.) To this day, the nickel coin is made of nickel—25 percent nickel, to be exact—and copper.

But let's return to wood for a moment. The reference to wooden nickels at the top of this entry might not be as preposterous as it seems. According to the Wooden Nickel Historical Museum, round wooden coins were issued in the early 1930s by the chamber of commerce of Blaine, Washington, following the failure of a local bank. These wooden coins, which included nickels, are considered the first legal wooden money and are now valuable collector's items.

Of course, there's the well-known phrase, "Don't take any wooden nickels." This saying is believed to have originated in the early twentieth century when commemorative wooden tokens, about the shape and size of nickels, were sometimes issued as currency to be used at exhibitions or fairs. Once the event closed, the "coins" became worthless, leaving owners of any unused wooden nickels feeling as if they'd been scammed.

Q How many Bibles are stolen from hotel rooms?

A You can bank on finding several items in a typical hotel room: stationary, tiny bottles of shampoo, and the Bible. Said Bible was probably placed in the nightstand drawer by a member of The Gideons International, a nondenominational Christian men's organization. The Gideons have placed more than 1.4 billion Bibles in hotel rooms (as well as in prisons, hospitals, schools, and other locations) since 1908.

Anyone staying in the hotel room is free to peruse the Bible. The Gideons find out when a new hotel has opened and approach management to ask if they can place Bibles in rooms at no cost to the hotel. Membership fees, donations, and evangelical churches fund their mission. After placing the Bibles, the Gideons usually return periodically to replace missing or damaged books.

According to the Gideons, there's no cause for concern if a Bible is taken from a hotel room. in fact, some prefer to avoid using the word "stolen" altogether: They believe that if a traveler takes a Bible with him or her, it's a good thing—it could mean that the person is on the path to becoming a Christian.

The Gideons claim that about 25 percent of travelers actually read these Bibles and that each Bible lasts, on average, for six years. In 2007, the Gideons distributed 70.7 million Bibles—that's more than 134 per minute. Although they do not track exactly how many are replaced because another Bible was taken (they also replace worn or damaged Bibles), these would seem to account for a significant portion of substitutions.

Some hotels have declined to have Gideons' Bibles placed in their rooms, instead offering a variety of religious texts upon request. On the flip side, a few hotels have begun offering "intimate" items, such as condoms (presumably, at a cost). So depending on where you stay, you may find a condom where you expect to see a Bible. It gives an entirely different meaning to the concept of salvation.

Q Do libraries put the Bible in the fiction or nonfiction section?

A Walk into just about any library in the United States and ask for a copy of the Bible. Without hesitation, the librarian will point to the reference section and say, "It's under B." Most libraries do not place the Bible in the fiction *or* nonfiction section—the Bible is typically considered adult reference or just plain reference material.

There are exceptions. If a library has more than one copy of the Bible, it will place one in reference and the extras in nonfiction, where patrons can check them out. (Reference materials can't be checked out of any library. The Bible has a permanent place in the reference section because it is considered a heavily used book, much like its neighbor the encyclopedia.)

That said, there is a system for classifying the Bible that's not based on how many copies a specific library branch may have. Like all other books, the Bible has a permanent place in the Dewey Decimal Classification System (DDC), widely used method for classifying books. The Bible is listed in the DDC religion section, which covers nine topics, beginning with natural theology and ending with comparative religions.

There you have it. We've just saved you from getting lost the next time you go to your friendly neighborhood library in search of the Bible. Kudos to us.

Q Does anyone use a number 1 pencil?

A Of course. Artists use number 1 pencils frequently because the soft lead produces dark lines and marks that are great for shading. You might also choose a number 1 pencil when you're writing something that is going to be faxed or photocopied.

Pencil leads come in different varieties, and here it's important to note that pencil lead is not lead at all—it's graphite, a mined mineral that's a form of carbon-like coal. Graphite is mixed with clay in various ratios to form the pencil core. More clay and less graphite creates a harder but lighter-colored core.

The types of cores, or leads, are rated according to their hardness (H) and blackness (B). A good old number 2 pencil, the most common type, is not quite as black as a number 1; a number 1 is softer and gets used up faster than a number 2. At the other end of the scale is the number 4 pencil, which is very hard but brittle and produces light marks that may be difficult to read.

These handy ratings may not be consistent among pencil manufacturers, or from country to country. In general, for example, European scales rank pencils from 9B, the blackest and softest, to 9H, the lightest and hardest. The number 2 pencil is rated in Europe as HB.

As for that number 1 pencil, its soft lead is useful to sketchers because the lines smudge and create shading. To an artist, that's good. To an engineer or architect, smudges are bad. These professionals use pencils for blueprints and drawings that must be exact, so they prefer a much harder pencil lead that draws a crisp, thin line.

Much like the beds of those three fairy tale bears, a number 1 might be too soft and a number 3 too hard, but a number 2 is juuuust right.

Q Is youth wasted on the young?

A Here's a little test. When you read this question, did you:

a) Yell out, "Yes!" in a loud, unsettling voice, causing all the people around you—on the bus, in the bookstore, or wherever you are—to stare at you like you're a raving lunatic?

b) Shrug your shoulders and wonder what the fuss is all about?

While you're waiting for the results of your test, here's some background: The late Irish playwright George Bernard Shaw is credited with a quote that goes something like this: "Youth is a wonderful thing. What a crime to waste it on children." The wit is pure Shaw, but the sentiment is universal and likely has been articulated in every culture and society throughout the history of mankind.

Time plays a cruel trick on all of us. As we trudge along on the inescapable path toward old age, we gain the wisdom to look back and recognize that we sometimes misspent the physical and emotional energy that was so plentiful in our youth. Older folks will tell you that if they could put their wiser, learned heads on their younger bodies, what great things they could accomplish! Languages and musical instruments learned, businesses launched and grown, novels written, miles jogged, good deeds done. Of course, most of these would-be accomplishments are pure B.S.: It's really mostly about sex, and maybe the ability to recover quickly from a hangover. The younger you are, the harder you can party.

And now, your test results. If you answered "a," you're probably forty or older. If you answered "b," you're definitely too young to understand.

Q Should you be carrying a firearm if you're riding shotgun?

A That depends. We need to know more about your workplace. Does your industry's list of trendy buzzwords include terms such as "reckon" and "yee-ha"? Do injuns and/

or bandits ever keep your team from meeting its goals and objectives? Does the food service staff consist of an ornery hombre named Cookie? If so, there's a good chance that you're employed by a stagecoach company, in which case the answer to this question would be yes. (Of course, there's also a pretty good chance that you're dead.)

In nineteenth-century America, the shotgun was the weapon of choice among stagecoach operators who had to travel through wild territory to complete their rounds. A guard armed with a shotgun would typically ride next to the stagecoach driver, ready to blast away at troublemakers who blocked their path.

Curiously, however, there is no evidence of the term "riding shotgun" being used to describe these armed guards. In fact, it appears that usage of the term didn't begin until the twentieth century—most likely first in pulp fiction stories about the Old West and subsequently in radio, films, and television, where Westerns were a programming staple from the 1930s through the 1950s. Along the way, the term worked itself into the popular lexicon as a way to describe riding in the passenger seat of a car.

Obviously, you don't need to be packing heat to ride shotgun today, but you can still re-live the glory days of the Old West if you so choose. Most states have right-to-carry laws that allow you to take a firearm with you when you drive, provided that you keep the gun concealed, have the proper permits, and haven't killed or robbed anybody lately.

Yee-ha!

Q What is the difference between four-wheel drive and all-wheel drive?

A Four-wheel drive (4WD) and all-wheel drive (AWD) vehicles have the same aim—to improve traction—but they go about it in different ways. Each has its advantages, and as some drivers discover when they are door-handle-deep in a snowdrift, neither is foolproof.

If your ride has 4WD or AWD, it's capable of transmitting engine power to all four tires, not just to the front tires (as in front-wheel-drive vehicles) or to the rear tires (as in rear-wheel-drive vehicles).

Traditional 4WD provides maximum pulling power and the ability to lock in a 50 percent front/50 percent rear power split. It also has separate gear ratios in order to multiply engine power in low speed, off-road conditions. And in many cases, the driver can choose between 2WD and 4WD with the yank of a floorboard lever or the twist of a dashboard knob.

AWD blends minimum hassle with the ability to automatically send power to the tires that can make the most of available grip. In normal conditions, power flows mostly through the front or rear wheels, depending on whether the vehicle is based on a front- or rear-wheel-drive design. If sensors detect any tires slipping due to a loss of traction, engine power is redistributed front to back or side to side to keep the vehicle moving. There's no low-range gearing, and the system is always on, so no action is required from the driver.

In general, 4WD is the province of heavier-duty SUVs and pickup trucks, which have separate bodies bolted to stout frames. AWD is the ticket for cars, minivans, and the new crop of lighter-duty "crossover" SUVs. These vehicles feature unibody construction, which integrates the frame with the vehicle's overall structure.

Four-wheel drive employs heavy mechanical hardware and, combined with the inherent weight of body-on-frame construction, signals that gas mileage isn't going to be great. AWD driveline components add some weight to a vehicle, but AWD saves pounds with electronic or fluid couplings. Combined with efficient unibody design, AWD is the choice for fuel efficiency.

Over the years, differences between the two systems have blurred. Most 4WD setups now mimic the versatile characteristics of AWD, and many AWD systems can imitate the grip-enhancing abilities of true 4WD.

Whereas once 4WD could not be employed on dry pavement for fear of damaging driveline components, today's best systems can remain engaged on any surface, and many boast the ability to dole out power front to back and left to right. The most sophisticated systems trade traditional low-range transfer cases for electronic traction-enhancers that enable vehicles to claw though off-road obstacles. Some AWD systems, meanwhile, can lock in a fifty/fifty power split, and others are engineered to enhance both off-road prowess and high-performance on-road handling.

It's worth noting that SUVs are often advertised or labeled as having 4WD, when they really have AWD; perhaps "four-wheel drive" sounds tougher on an SUV. And it's vital to understand that neither system can overcome the laws of physics. The traction magic that gets you going in snow or slop is powerless to keep you from sliding in a turn taken too fast or to stop you quickly on slippery pavement. If you have 4WD or AWD, beware of FSS—a False Sense of Security.

Q Why do men's and women's shirts have buttons on opposite sides?

A Despite the many strides the feminist movement has made over the past few decades, there is simply no denying that men and women are biologically different (except in certain red-light-district shows, which we've never, ever seen). Clothing has developed in ways to accommodate these differences. Some make sense (we'd wager that you've never seen women's underwear sporting that little flap/vent thing). But putting buttons on opposite sides of the shirt? Why?

Although it might seem ridiculous for men's and women's shirts to have buttons on opposite sides—most people are right-handed, and it is far easier to manipulate a button with your dominant hand—scholars point to fashion history to explain how this came to be.

Buttons have been around for thousands of years, but they served no purpose other than being decorative until about the thirteenth century. That's when the functional button (and just as importantly, the buttonhole) was invented, sending European nobility into a veritable button frenzy. Buttons became a symbol of both status and fashion, appearing everywhere and anywhere, often unnecessarily.

Perhaps the apex of button mania came in the sixteenth century with the button-loving king of France, Francis I. In 1520, Francis I planned a meeting with the English king, Henry VIII, in hopes of arranging a military alliance. Wanting desperately to impress Henry VIII, Francis I thought long and hard about how to strike the right chord.

It was the sort of situation that required the utmost tact and statesmanship; the sort of situation that needed the grace and intelligence befitting the ruler of one of the world's greatest powers; the sort of situation, Francis I tragically decided, that demanded he wear a velvet suit adorned with more than thirteen thousand gold buttons. There is no record of Henry VIII's reaction, though it goes without saying that no alliance was formed.

Francis I's ill-fated wardrobe decision also gives us insight into our original question. For a long time, buttons were too costly to appear on anything except the garments of the nobility. Because noble ladies were dressed by their servants, it was the obvious choice to put the buttons on the left side, making it easier for the right-handed servants to button their mistresses. Men dressed themselves, and so their buttons went on the right.

According to historians, there is no real reason for men's and women's buttons to persist in their opposition—it continues out of tradition. Thankfully, that's the only button tradition Francis I and his contemporaries bequeathed to us.

Q What's the difference between antiperspirant and deodorant?

A So many choices! No one wants to stink, and most people would just as soon not sweat. So which do you use: deodorant or antiperspirant?

The answer isn't quite as simple as you might think. Both are designed to eliminate body odor from under the arms, but they work differently. Deodorants let you sweat but contain fragrances that kill foul smells; antiperspirants clog pores to stop sweat from emerging in the first place. Sweat is actually odorless; it's mostly water and salt. It does, however, attract bacteria. The bacteria feed on sweat and break it down, which generates the stink we all want to avoid.

Stick deodorants control the smell of body odor by turning the skin acidic. You'll still sweat, but the bacteria that thrive on sweat stay away, so you don't smell bad. In fact, since most deodorants contain perfume, you smell pretty good. Deodorants are considered cosmetics.

Antiperspirants, however, are drugs, since they change the body's physiology. Antiperspirants use aluminum-based compounds to plug up pores, stop sweat, and keep skin dry. The most recent antiperspirant compound is aluminum zirconium tetrachlorohydrex glycine—just trying to spell that correctly would make anyone sweat!

Deodorants—in the forms of perfumes and fragrances—have been around for thousands of years. Antiperspirants are newcomers to the marketplace, though. The first antiperspirant was called

Everdry; it hit American drugstore shelves in 1903. Nowadays, most antiperspirants contain deodorant as well—but not the other way around.

In any event, be thankful for antiperspirant and deodorant. They haved saved us from reeking, and what could be better than that?

Q How do they get a model ship into a bottle?

A You ask very nicely and tell it to suck in its gut, of course. People have been putting stuff in empty bottles for centuries. Before ships caught on, "patience bottles" were filled with scenes of religious imagery (Jesus on the cross, for example), and aptly named "mining bottles" had multilevel scenes of ore mining. The earliest mining bottle, which dates to 1719, was created by Matthias Buchinger, a well-known entertainer of the time who had no arms or legs. Mining bottles originated in what is now Hungary.

People started shoving ships into bottles in the mid- to late eighteenth century. Most people did not write the dates on their creations, and since many were made with old bottles that had been sitting around, the date on the actual bottle doesn't necessarily mean that's when the ship was put in it. The earliest ship in a bottle that someone bothered to date (on the sails) was constructed in 1784. Bottling ships really caught on in the 1830s, when clear glass became more common. It is still a popular hobby these days, with clubs and associations around the world devoted to the skill.

But how do you get that boat into the bottle? It's actually pretty simple (not easy, but simple). The hull (or bottom of the boat) is narrow enough to fit through the neck of the bottle. The masts are hinged so that they can be pushed flat against the hull. While the ship is outside the bottle, the sails are attached and a string is tied to the mast. The masts and sails are bent so that they are flat, and then the whole thing is pushed through the bottleneck. Glue or putty on the bottom of the bottle keeps the ship anchored. Once the ship is in, a long tool, shaped like a rod or skewer, is used to position it. Finally, the string that is attached to the masts is pulled to bring up the sails and complete the illusion.

There are some types of boats—motorboats, for example—that are too wide to get into the bottle in one piece. These are assembled inside the bottle using rods, which takes a lot of patience and a steady hand.

Getting a ship out of a bottle? Easy—navigate it toward an iceberg or a jagged rock.

Q Are highway weigh stations ever open?

A Nothing highlights the true diversity of landscapes, peoples, and cultures in the melting pot of these United States better than a cross-country drive. And no matter where you are in this great land, it's comforting to know that you can rely on one thing: Whenever you come upon a weigh station on the side of the interstate, it will be closed.

Even though their erratic hours of operation may not indicate as much, highway weigh stations are an important part of the nation's transportation infrastructure. Created in the first part of the twentieth century to help collect transportation taxes, weigh stations now exist primarily to ensure that big rigs aren't over the legal weight limit. Each state is required to run its own weigh stations, but this task generally isn't too high on the list of law-enforcement priorities.

Most states suffer from shortages of law-enforcement personnel, so it's no surprise that officers who man weigh stations are among the first to be reassigned to areas with more pressing needs. Due to personnel shortages, many states have opted to implement a plan that opens weigh stations at random times (though in bureaucratese, "random" apparently means "never").

Sometimes weigh stations are closed because of technical issues. In New Jersey, for example, a lot of taxpayers wondered why the state spent fifty-four million dollars on a high-tech weigh station that never seemed to be in operation. The answer most likely didn't please anyone. Besides the usual problems of being short-staffed—apparently, fifty-four million dollars doesn't go as far as it used to—this high-tech facility was closed for a significant period of time because mice ate through fiber-optic cables that control the sensors. Perhaps the few dozen bucks it would have cost to buy mousetraps would have knocked the project over budget.

Q What's the difference between a tomb, a crypt, a sepulcher, and a sarcophagus?

A It's all about perspective. Today, going out in style is retiring to a house that has a fishing boat docked a hundred feet from the front door. Centuries ago, people looked at things a bit differently. Forget cozy cottages and rainbow trout—we're talking gold-plated resting places for your bones in the afterlife. Now that's going out in style, gentle reader.

People once had to tackle decisions on tombs, sarcophagi, crypts, and sepulchers that make today's debate over whether to splurge on the cherry casket for Grandma seem pretty straightforward. What's the difference between these burial places?

Let's start with the easy one. A tomb can be something as simple as a hole in the ground, but it typically refers to a structure or vault for interment below or above ground. It can also mean a memorial shrine above a grave—a tradition that may have humbly started in prehistoric times, when families buried their dead underneath their dwellings. In the Middle Ages, Christian tombs became breathtaking structures that sometimes saw entire churches built over the graves of departed dignitaries. In 1066, for example, King Edward the Confessor was entombed in front of the high altar at Westminster Abbey in Great Britain.

A crypt is a specific type of tomb, usually a vault or chamber built beneath a church. Outstanding servants of a particular church—bishops, for example, or extremely loyal parishioners—are often buried in the crypt under a church. Centuries ago in Europe, these vast burial chambers also served as meeting places. We suspect, however, that no one held Christmas parties in them.

A sepulcher is another old-timey word for a tomb or place of burial. It often describes tombs carved out of rock or built from stone. Usually when the word "sepulcher" is thrown around, it's in reference to the tomb in which Jesus was laid to rest, a sepulcher near Calvary. The reputed site is commemorated by the Church of the Holy Sepulchre, which was dedicated in the fourth century, destroyed and rebuilt several times, and is now visited by thousands of tourists every year.

Finally, a sarcophagus is a bit different from the other three burial places we've described in that the term generally refers to an elaborate casket that isn't sunk into the ground. The oldest are from Egypt, box-shaped with separate lids; later Egyptian sarcophagi were often shaped like the body. The most famous sarcophagus holds Egypt's Tutankhamen, better known as King Tut. Discovered in 1922, it is made of quartzite, has reliefs of goddesses carved into the sides, and sports a heavy granite lid.

In today's world, the good ol' hole in the ground is the most popular burial choice. After that retirement house on the lake has been paid off, there isn't enough money left to do up death King Tut-style.

Q Why are people afraid of clowns?

A Got a case of coulrophobia? You're not alone. Experts estimate that as many as one in seven people suffer from an abnormal or exaggerated fear of clowns. The symptoms of this strangely common affliction range from nausea and sweating to irregular heartbeat, shortness of breath, and an overall feeling of impending doom. Is the sight of Ronald McDonald more chilling than your Chocolate Triple Thick Shake? There could be a few reasons why.

The most common explanation for coulrophobia is that the sufferer had a bad experience with a clown at a young and impressionable age. Maybe the clown at Billy Schuster's fifth birthday party shot you in the eye with a squirting flower, doused your head with confetti, or accidentally popped the balloon animal he was making for you. Some of the most silly or mundane things can be petrifying when you are young. And though the incident may be long forgotten, a bright orange wig or bulbous red nose might be enough to throw you back into the irrational fears that plagued your younger days.

Who could blame you? If television and movies have taught us anything, it's that clowns often are creatures of pure evil. There's the Joker, Batman's murderously insane archenemy; the shapeshifting Pennywise from Stephen King's *It;* the human-eating alien clowns in *Killer Klowns from Outer Space;* and a possessed toy clown that comes to life and beats the bejesus out of a young Robbie Freeling in Steven Spielberg's *Poltergeist.*

Real-life serial killer John Wayne Gacy didn't do much for the clown cause, either. Before authorities found the bodies of twenty-seven boys and young men in his basement crawl space, Gacy was known as a charming, sociable guy who enjoyed performing at children's parties dressed up as Pogo the Clown or Patches the Clown. That ended when his crimes were discovered, but even on death row he still had an unwholesome interest in clowning—he took up oil painting, and clowns were his favorite subjects.

It's enough to give anyone the heebie-jeebies. But some experts say there's more to coulrophobia than traumatic childhood events or pop-culture portrayals. Scholar Joseph Durwin points out that since ancient times, clowns, fools, and jesters have been given permission to mock, criticize, or act deviantly and unexpectedly. This freedom to behave outside of normal social boundaries is exactly what makes clowns so threatening.

A *Nursing Standard* magazine interview of 250 people ages four to sixteen revealed that clowns are indeed "universally scary." Researcher Penny Curtis reported some kids found clowns to be "quite frightening and unknowable." Seems it has a lot to do with that permanent grease-painted grin. Because the face of a clown never changes, you don't know if he's relentlessly gleeful or about to bite your face off. In the words of Bart Simpson: "Can't sleep; clown will eat me."

CONTRIBUTORS

Diane Lanzillotta Bobis is a food, fashion, and lifestyle writer living in Glenview, Illinois.

Jack Greer is a writer living in Chicago.

Joshua D. Boeringa is a writer living in Mt. Pleasant, Michigan. He has written for magazines and Web sites.

Vickey Kalambakal is a writer and historian based in Southern California. She writes for textbooks, encyclopedias, magazines, and ezines.

Brett Kyle is a writer living in Draycott, Somerset, England. He also is an actor, musician, singer, and playwright.

Anthony G. Craine is a contributor to the *Britannica Book of the Year* and has written for *Inside Sports* and *Ask* magazines. He is a former United Press International bureau chief.

Alex Nechas is a writer and editor based in Chicago.

ArLynn Leiber Presser is a writer living in suburban Chicago. She is the author of twenty-seven books.

Pat Sherman is the author of several books for children, including *The Sun's Daughter* and *Ben and the Proclamation of Emancipation*.

Carrie Williford is a writer living in Atlanta. She was a contributing writer to HowStuffWorks.com.

Thad Plumley is an award-winning writer who living in Dublin, Ohio. He is the director of publications and information products for the National Ground Water Association.

Letty Livingston is a dating coach, relationship counselor, and sexpert. Her advice column, Let Letty Help, is available on the Internet (letlettyhelp.blogspot.com).

Noah Liberman is a Chicago-based sports, entertainment, and business writer who has published two books and has contributed articles to newspapers and magazines.

Michelle Burton is a writer and editor living in both Chicago and Newport Beach, California. She has written guidebooks, feature articles, and reviews.

Steve Cameron is a writer living in Cullen, Scotland. He has written thirteen books, and is a former columnist and reporter for several American newspapers and magazines.

Shanna Freeman is a writer and editor living near Atlanta. She works in an academic library.

Chuck Giametta is a highly acclaimed journalist who specializes in coverage of the automotive industry. He has written and edited books, magazines, and Web articles on many automotive topics.

Tom Harris is a Web project consultant, editor, and writer living in Atlanta. He is the co-founder of Explainst.com, and was head of the editorial content team at HowStuffWorks.com.

Angelique Anacleto specializes in style and beauty writing. She has written for salon industry publications and has authored a children's book.

Dan Dalton is a writer and editor living in the Pacific Northwest.

Jessica Royer Ocken is a writer and editor based in Chicago.

Brett Ballantini is a sportswriter who has written for several major sports teams and has authored a book titled *The Wit and Wisdom of Ozzie Guillen*.

Ed Grabianowski writes about science, nature, history, the automotive industry, and science fiction for Web sites and magazines. He lives in Buffalo, New York.

Jeff Moores is an illustrator whose work appears in periodicals and advertisements and as licensed characters on clothing. Visit his Web site (jeffmoores.com) to see more of his work.

Factual verification: Darcy Chadwick, Barbara Cross, Bonny M. Davidson, Andrew Garrett, Cindy Hangartner, Brenda McLean, Carl Miller, Katrina O'Brien, Marilyn Perlberg